The Art of Decryption in the 17th century

version 2. 2022

Translated from French: L'art de deschiffrer. Traité de déchiffrement du XVIIe siècle de la Secrétairerie d'Etat et de Guerre Espagnole, 1668 – 1714. Published in French 1967 by J.P. Devos, H. Seligman. Université De Louvain.

LEUIA HIC VERBULA EXPOLIT

Source: Jacob de Zetter 1620. Wolfenbüttel Herzog August Bibliothek.

Let's sharpen our mind with language!

Contents

Translator's preface

The article in the Cryptologia[1] where this small book was described states:

> "The most detailed and didactic handbook of code breaking from that time, the anonymous Art de deschiffrer, a 136-page handbook written in French in the 17th century."

Browsing through the Internet showed that it was mentioned [2] on some places and after the purchase of the digital version of the book, I tried to read it. The French text is constructed by long paragraphs with persistent double negations, which are very difficult to comprehend. In the period it was written those long lines showed that the author had a particular intellectual knowledge. But nowadays, we are used to short lines, quick tweets and icons and we are not used to read long paragraphs anymore. We need short bits and quick bites. Thus, the text looked at me and I looked back, and I started translating.

Because there is almost no information on how to approach the decryption of an unknown homophonic cipher, every source is important. There are some medieval unsolved cryptograms that probably use such a method. Some of those unsolved ones are the Rohonc manuscript and the Voynich manuscript. Although some people may argue that it has not been determined that these manuscripts contain such methods and may not be a cipher.

The text from *L'Art de deschiffrer* has an anonymous author and originates from around the years 1668-1714. This period could be determined based on the used text for the examples inside. The manuscript was first discovered and edited by DEVOS and SELIGMAN and published in 1967, again in French.

Sometimes the construction of the sentences is complex, and I always tried to avoid long sentences, but the original text does not always provide the best opportunity to do so: original sentences can be half a page long, and it was

---

[1] Láng, Benedek(2010) 'Why Don't We Decipher an Outdated Cipher System? The Codex of Rohonc',
Cryptologia, 34: 2, 115 — 144 . URL: http://dx.doi.org/10.1080/01611191003605587.
Online publication date: 05 April 2010 (DS)
[2] Site: http://cryptiana.web.fc2.com/code/louisxiv0.htm : Ciphers Early in the Reign of Louis XIV. (DS)

often too difficult to cut them up into smaller pieces and to maintain the same explanation. Also, by cutting up every sentence in smaller pieces, the spirit of the original would be lost and that was not what I wanted. I hope that this old knowledge on the art of decryption will be of help during the decryption of the unknown and older ciphers.

Some remarks:
* I've added some footnotes to the text, these can be recognized by the marking (DS)
* In the Appendix you will find background statistics on the "Nijmegen cipher" from my hand
* The notes inside the text that look like (1vo) (44vo) etc. refer to the original folio numbers in the manuscript
* My translated version originally published in 2019, has been changed and uploaded to Amazon in 2022 and is now the current version you are reading

David Scheers.

- - - - - - - - - - -- - - - - -- - - - -- - - - - - - -- - - - -- - - - -- - - - - - - -- - - - -- - - - - - -- - - - -- - - - - -- - - - -- - - - - - -

The original front cover from 1967 shows the following information:
Université De Louvain, Recueil De Travaux D'histoire Et De Philologie, 4e Série, Fascicule 36. Original title: L'art de deschiffrer. Traité de déchiffrement du XVIIe siècle de la Secrétairerie d'Etat et de Guerre Espagnole. édité par J.P. Devos, D. Ph. L. professeur honoraire à l'Athénée Royal de Louvain, et H. Seligman, Lieutenant Général E.R. de l'Armée Belge. Louvain. 1967.

- What now follows is the translated text -

Summary

THE ART OF DECRYPTION (1967)

According to cryptologists, it's a rare find to discover something written on decryption.
Because on the one hand the job of cipherer was not without danger - one could be accused of magic or witchcraft - and on the other hand one did not want to unveil the secrets of such profitable art.

This treatise is titled <u>The Art of DECRYPTION</u> and it contains writings of three different hands, dated between the years 1668 and 1714.

The text contains principles of decryption used in the seventeenth century, and it contains good deciphering techniques and is therefore interesting in more than one respect.

It gives us a glance of the modus operandi of the army and the chancelleries (encryption departments of governments) which always remain unknown and obscure through times by its very nature.

Introduction

It's a real luxury to discover a deciphering treatise. Renowned cryptologists such as Alois Meister, and I recommend Bazeries, A. Lange and E.A. Soudart, unanimously affirm that this kind of document is very rare. [3]
This explains, because the profession of cipherer was not without danger, one could be accused of either witchcraft or magic like J.B. Porta [4], and on the other

---

[3] A. MEISTER, Die Geheimschrift im Dienste der Piipstlichen Kurie, Paxder- bom, 1906, p. 45; Die Anfiinge der modernen diplomatischen Geheimschrift, Paderborn, 1902, Introduction.
Commandant BAZERIES, Les Chiffres secrets dévoilés, Paris, 1901, p. 42. LANGE et SouDART, Traité de Cryptographie, Paris, 1925, Introduction, p. V-VI, p. 26-27.
[4] Here the Italian scientist Giovanni Battista della Porta is mentioned. Although he was examined by the inquisition some years before 1570, and there were implications on the publication of his work, he remained under life-long surveillance by the inquisition. See <u>Stanford encyclopedia.</u> (DS)

hand one did not want to reveal the secrets of the art which brought with them honour and profit.

Rich archives such as the Vatican and the Venice Chancellery contain only a small number of these treaties. [5] And during our visit of the Archive General of Simancas, we discovered that it did not have any such document.
The treatise we publish is titled: L'Art de Deschiffrer (Art of Decryption). It belongs to the General Archives of the Kingdom in Brussels, where it is classified under number 3 in the Secretary of State and War.

Manuscript form

It is a collection of 83 sheets of white laid paper, the first 15 are foliated. They are contained in a modern binding, which is quite different. It measures 215 mm X 305 mm.

Conservation state

The first 13 leaflets contain the first treatise (**A**). This text is preserved well, but it has a set of irrelevant considerations from the viewpoint of cryptography.

The two following pages contain a note, the text (**B**) of which refers to the second treatise (**C**). The upper part has obviously suffered from humidity, the writing is so pale that in some places it almost disappeared. The upper edges were deeply wounded by rodents and worms, which made many large holes. Some restauration with transparent paper did not help to preserve the writing. On the contrary, by using glue, some words have become completely illegible.

Concerning the second treatise (**C**), it contains 68 pages that are numbered. This is the most important part of the manuscript. They are well preserved, but the writing is very pale. In many places the text is still barely readable. In some years it will be completely gone and will become illegible. Then this rare document, a precious pearl in our Archive, will be lost for the study of Cryptography.

---

[5] It is the same at the Quai d'Orsay (Letter from the Head of the Department of Archives of Foreign Affairs, March 3, 1933). (Lettre du chef du Service des Archives des Affaires Étrangères, 3 mars 1933).

By careful reading, the disappearance of the leaflets between sheets 30 and 31 have been discovered. They seem to have formed the preamble of chapter V. The writing, from three different hands, is between the second half of the seventeenth and the beginning of the eighteenth century.

The French language used by the editor is from the same period. However, the style and spelling reveal the author's Spanish roots. This is evident in the Treatise (Traitté) and the inserted passages which are in this language and are from someone who knows Castilian [6] very well.

Some French words are written according to the rules of the Spanish language, eg. "verd", in Spanish "verde" (see the text, page 5v). The text reveals that the author is a person devoted to the Spanish Crown. This treatise, which has never been published, was once subject of further study performed by H. Seligman.[7] Nor can we forget the predecessors of cryptanalysis, the eminent French cryptologists and French Hispanists. [8]

It is the second text (**C**) that is by far the most important that is now published, viewing it from practical and systematic angle.

The content of the manuscript makes it possible to locate, with certainty, the original composition lies between the years 1668 and 1714. In the history of Cryptography, this document lies between "L'Interpretation des chiffres" by Cospi (1641), the works of Breithaupt (1737) and Conrad (1739), from the early eighteenth century.

The importance of this second text is increased because at this time we do not know of any similar text, not even in France; the use of ciphers appears to be neglected. [9]

---

[6] Castilian Spanish refers to Spanish spoken as a whole. Castellano (Castilian) can refer to that, but also to medieval Old Spanish language, which is a predecessor to modern Spanish. (DS)

[7] H. Séligman (1868-1955, lieutenant, général e.r. de l'Armée Belge), Un traité de déchiffrement du XVJJe siècle, dans Revue des Bibliothèques et Archives de Belgique, t. VI, 1908, pp. 1-19.

[8] e.a. MM. E. Dhorme et M. Bataillon, membres de l'Institut de France.

[9] Lange et Soudart, op. cil., p. 45-46, 54-55.

This unique second treatise contains principles of deciphering applied to the ciphers of the seventeenth century in the secret chancelleries, and the second part is a good deciphering treatise and is truly remarkable.

The text is entitled "Treatise on the art of decryption" [10], and is 68 double-sided pages in the manuscript. As we have observed previously, it bears neither date, nor author's name. The author seems to be well skilled in cryptography and appears to have been in touch with the Madrid Court Service. He gives an example of decryption of a fragment of an encrypted letter, of which he had the original in his hands and which was sent by the ambassadors of Louis XIV in Nijmegen (the Netherlands) and had been intercepted in 1676 by the Spanish.

Consequently, the author must have been in the service of the King of Spain, and it may be admitted that he wrote his work between 1676 and 1714, the date of the Treaty of Rastadt.[11]

In a brief introduction, he tends to show that the art of deciphering is the most difficult of all. Each art, he says, is based on well-established principles, while the cryptologist [12] has no basis; he works in the unknown. Also today, cryptography is for some authors a special art, because the practise requires special skills, which is true, but also exhaustive encyclopedic knowledge, which is exaggerated.

It is understandable that this exaggeration is found in our author, who belongs to the seventeenth century, at a time when the sciences were experiencing a period of extraordinary growth.
After having introduced the parts of his work, he finishes with these words: [13]

"And finally, we will deal with indecipherable ciphers with which we will finish this work, whose defects seem to deserve all the more indulgence as the one who commits them, walks in a path that he opened himself and engages a road that he does not believe has been stepped on by anyone yet."

———————————————————

[10] Original: "Traité de l'Art de deschiffrer" (DS)
[11] The peace Treaty of Rastatt between France and Austria on 7 March 1714 in the city of Rastatt. A full list can be found on https://en.wikipedia.org/wiki/List_of_treaties (DS)
[12] cryptographer (DS)
[13] «Et enfin l'on traitera des chiffres indéchiffrables par où l'on finira cet ouvrage dont les défauts semblent mériter d'autant plus d'indulgence que celui qui les commet, marche dans un chemin qu'il s'est ouvert lui même et s'engage dans une route qu'il ne croit pas avoir encor été frayée par personne» (DS)

This confirms our opinion on the scarcity of deciphering treaties currently, and authorizes us perhaps, to assume that the author did not know about Porta's work: "De occultis literarum nolis" (Montbéliard, 1593) and "De Jurtivis literarum notis" (Naples 1563 and 1602, Strasbourg 1603, 1606 and 1616), as well as the cipher interpretation of Cospi (1641).

As the cryptologists and officials of ciphers always avoided publication of their procedures outside the uninitiated circles, we believe that our author has complied with this practice and confines himself to this great secrecy of ciphering. Nowadays, little is known in the methods of post-war ciphers 1914-1918 and even almost nothing is known about the cryptography used from 1940 to 1945. [14]

The chapters

We will now briefly examine the various chapters of the composed work.

- Chapter I: "General Principles on the Art of Decryption".
  The author defines a cipher as follows: "The cipher is nothing else - to speak in terms of The School – only a third mediator between the thoughts of men, that regulates and conducts between two or more persons, to make their feelings known to another by writing and to disguise these to those who are not part of the ministry". It is to the "terms of The School" that he attributes the pedantry of this definition. [15] The general principles in this chapter postulate that each language has its peculiar behaviour, the one who wants to decrypt, must limit himself in the beginning to a small number of characters, the one that are most frequent, whose discovery will lead to discovery of all other characters. This chapter, written in pompous and bombastic style, contains unnecessary digressions.

- Chapter II includes the specific principles on the Art of Decryption, with the following definitions:

---

[14] Lange et Soudart, op. cit., p. 92-284 + Errata p, V.
[15] L'Escole = School. Here the philosophical school is meant as a general teaching entity "The School" as Scholasticism. (DS)

* Simple cipher = one that expresses only the letters of the alphabet.
* Composite cipher = containing coding of letters, syllables, half words, and whole words, such as those commonly used in chancelleries.
* Regular cipher = where characters always express the same thing.
* Irregular cipher = numbers change in meaning depending on places and contacts.

The author says that we must first find out what kind of cipher we are dealing with, then rank the various signs used and count their strength. The current cryptographic vocabulary uses the term "frequency analysis" for this. Then we must try to discover the null, without working too hard on the thing, because the knowledge on other characters will inevitably reveal the nulls.

- In chapter III, the author presents the method of deciphering simple ciphers in both Spanish and French. This chapter includes a series of axioms and rules. The axioms give the frequencies of the letters and bigrams as well as which peculiarities there are concerning polygrams[16]. The given rules show peculiarities in languages and will facilitate the discovery of the vowels as well as certain letters, certain words, and procedures to check the accuracy of the first hypotheses made.
One will find all the elements necessary to decipher cryptograms of the period, encrypted by a monogrammatic substitution system. We show these observations because they are the outline of the rules defined at the end of the nineteenth century by captain Valerio, about the separation of vowels and particularities of liquids [17] L. and R. [18] This fact demonstrates that the author is a forerunner of modern cryptography; he also shows he is a master of Spanish encryption systems. "Never more than five consonants can follow each other immediately and rarely there are more than four. Take into account that the vowels are more

---

[16] Also known as multigram (French polygramme, multigramme) such as bigram, trigram, quadrigram, etc. (DS)

[17] In phonetics, liquids are a class of consonants consisting of voiced lateral approximants like /l/ together with rhotics like /r/. wikipedia (DS)

[18] Cap. P. VALERIO, De la Cryptographie, Paris, 1e Vol, 1893, 2e Vol, 1896. The NSA reported in 1942 they only then translated this text, and others. See here. I did not investigate this further (DS)

mingled with the entire text, when one finds a vowel between two consonants, that is to say, in the most repeated ciphered characters placed in between others which are less frequent, are inevitably vowels. To recognize R., both in French and in Spanish, look for the character which often follows a consonant *br, cr, dr, fr, gr*, and in the same situation *bl, cl* ".

- The chapter IV: "Application of the axioms and the rules that have been defined", provides two examples of deciphering two dispatches[19], one Spanish, the other French. They have been encrypted using an easy cipher.

- We cannot reproduce the title of chapter V because a sheet is missing between the 30th and the 31st page.
A piece of the missing text is preserved at the beginning of the 31st page, is the end of the original text. We can there see that it included general considerations on composite ciphers. [20] The author makes sixteen observations concerning the composite ciphers. They form the body of chapter V. There it shows the differences that characterize the repetitions and peculiarities of the language depending on a simple cipher or a composite one. [21]

All these observations complete the examination of the linguistic properties made during the study of simple ciphers. They concern especially the deciphering of the composite ciphers. (folio 1°).
Others are more general and still find their application in the decryption of encrypted dispatches with the help of dictionaries still in use today. For example, we cite an example that concerns the examination of

---

[19] Ciphered letters (DS)
[20] Note to Chapter V: There is a major gap in the text because of the disappearance of a page which was to constitute the preamble of chapter V. The surviving text contains 16 observations concerning the composite ciphers. In addition, the sheet (31) has a large tear that removed a significant portion of the last four lines of the text. (DS)
[21] They look like the current encrypted codes used during trade. The construction of the ciphers have been studied in Chapter IV: "The Spanish ciphers during the second half of the eighteenth century ", in our work: The cipher of Philip II (1555- 1598) *"Les chiffres de Philippe II "* and *"et du Despacho Universa/ durant le XVIIe siècle "* Despacho Universa / during the seventeenth century (Royal Academy of Belgium, Mém. In-4 °), Brussels, 1950.

ciphers that represent whole words: "However one can come to the same end another way, because it is only necessary to observe the numbers which are repeated the least in a letter and which are without being nulls are joined with others with which one notices that they cannot make any connection to form a word, because these are then whole words themselves, especially when they follow certain rules for such ciphers, which one can conclude by signalling words like he, she, the, of, etc ... "(12th observation).

- In chapter VI, among the "particular principles that facilitate the art of decryption" - such is its title - we note: "These remarks are very important and it is due to their efforts that we have discovered the encrypted letter which was sent to the Netherlands, and took two years by the Secretary of State and by order of His Majesty to experience the art which is the subject of this treatise". (2nd precept).
  This fact is of paramount importance because it tells us that cryptographic systems were tested before being adopted. It demonstrates the good organization of the encryption service the "Despacho Universal", as well as the practical value of this treatise.

- Chapter VII shows applying the rules concerning composite ciphers; the decipherment of two dispatches, one Spanish and the other French, is discussed in detail.
  The last two chapters are dedicated to cryptographic systems that do not require the use of ciphering tables.

- Chapter VIII is titled "Decryption method for certain ciphers". The author discusses the method of regular divisors used during that cryptographic time character by character. He gives the following description:
  "The key consist of a geometric figure like a square, a parallelogram, a triangle, etc., divide it into as many cells as one wants, and in each cell one puts in the letters based on ranking which form the message one wants to send, then take another figure and turn it and write on the other side, all characters in the same order of the new side of the figure that changes their arrangement so much that one does not recognize much more then only some gibberish." [22]

To decipher it without a key, the author advises the construction of a rectangle containing a very large number of cells. Then try to replace the letters 2 by 2, 3 by 3, etc., until we arrive at a series of letters forming a word in the opposite direction to that of the inscription.

- Chapter IX refers to a "Decryption method for a special cipher". It is the square cipher, used sometimes in Holland, writes the author.

  This cipher is the square table of Vigenère or double substitution cipher, in which the letters are replaced by numbers. [23] Father Kircher used this also in his book Polygraphia Universalis and published an "abacus numeralis", a square cipher table.[24]

  The horizontal alphabet represents the text in "clear" and the vertical alphabet indicates the key used to crypt the text. The author adds: "These kinds of ciphers are not very much used in the Secretary because of their length and the time it takes a person to encrypt and decipher a letter."
  The square cipher, as it was called, was long considered to be uncrackable. It was the German major Kasiski, who first provided a method in 1863 for decryption of double-key systems.[25]

- Chapter X is the last one with "Indecipherable ciphers", the author describes ciphers he has constructed and which he presents as indecipherable. The first is called "How to Encrypt by Addition and Subtraction"[26]. Here is the principle: we write under the letters of the alphabet the sequence of numbers from 1 to 22.

A	B	C	D	E	F	G	H	I	L	M	N	O	P	Q	R	S	T	V	X	Y	Z
1	2	3	4	5	6	7	8	9	10	11	12	13	14	15	16	17	18	19	20	21	22

---

[22] The original French word used here was: galimatias (DS)
[23] This table is reproduced in the edition of the manuscript. The "Despacho Universal", under Philip II, already knew the square cipher. Cfr J. P. DEvos, op. cit.
[24] Rome, 1663
[25] LANGE et SOUDART, op. cit. p. 163
[26] «Manière de chiffrer par addi- tion et soustraction»

Then "we agree on a sentence, a phrase, a passage from the Holy Scripture or a formula of daily prayers such as Pater Noster, Ave Maria, etc., which take the place of a key ". We then have the characters of this formula above those of the plain text that we want to encrypt, we make an addition of the two numbers representing the letters in each column and the result gives the cipher text for each character.

key	P	A	T	E	R	N	O	S	T	E	R	Q	V	I	E	S	T
plain text	L	A	R	M	E	E	E	S	T	E	N	M	A	R	C	H	E
cipher text	24	2	34	16	21	17	18	34	36	10	28	26	20	25	8	25	23

To decipher, we subtract from each number the corresponding number of the letter of the key, we thus find the numbers corresponding to the letters of the speech to be quantified.
This system resembles the so-called "the sum of Gronsfeld" process[27]. Let us say at once that he is only known because he was mentioned in a quote at the hand of P. Schott in his "Magia Universalis" published at Nuremberg in 1659. [28]

This process is a perfected version of the square of Vigenère without the help of a table and by transformation of the literal key into a numerical key with three or four digits.
The author of the "Treatise of the Art of Decryption" also perfected the square cipher by introducing the indefinite key, which is an improvement. This method is still in use in the systems of Beaufort (1857) and St-Cyr (1880).

The second cipher built by the author belongs to the so-called "directory" systems. It consists of a table of all possible combinations of two and three letters, and it represents each by a number of 3 digits (from 100 to 900).[29]

---

[27] Johann Franz Graf Gronsfeld-Bronkhorst (†1719) cipher (DS)
[28] It is GASPAR Schott, from the Society of Jesus, born in Koeningshofen (Augsburg) in 1608, first professor of philosophy and mathematics in Palermo, then in Augsburg, where he died in 1666. He published that year- his book "Schola Steganographica". His namesake and confrere was the famous Antwerp humanist André Schott (1552-1629).
[29] The author probably understands by "possible combinations", those that are usual,

To decipher, one must transcribe all the numbers corresponding to the text previously divided into bigrams and trigrams, then copy the dispatch separating the sequence of numbers to form groups of two and three digits.

cipher text	124. 256. 454. 113. 414. 553. 364. 785. 256...
transcribed	12.42.564. 541. 13. 41.4.55.33. 64.78. 52.56...
separated in groups	12.4 / 2.56 / 4.54 / 1.13 / 41.4 / 55.3 / 3.64 / 78.5 /2.56 ...

This system requires secrecy because if the enemy has the coding table, he can use the system.

This kind of cipher is an auxiliary method of decryption and not a proper cipher in the sense of the word. However, many commercial dictionaries of our era hardly rely on more solid processes than those used by our author.

In conclusion, he stated that he was not in favour of the use of these two kinds of ciphers in the Secretariats of States because they were too long and not practical when ciphering large text in dispatches; furthermore, the conversion of a single number poses the correspondent who holds the key for an impossible deciphering job. His preferences seem to go to earlier systems, including cipher tables and clean words. He develops throughout his reflexions the following conclusions:

"We can still imagine other ciphers, but they all have the same deficiencies, they seem to be superfluous when we try to make an accurate search especially in a text which is more to satisfy the curiosity of mind than it is for real practical use. Also, instead of attempting to compose extraordinary meta-physical ciphers, which are not good during use, it will always be better in the Secretaries the cipher tables and proper words, on which we must take care we make them more complete than usual, and increase the number of syllables for three letters, and use many nulls, and assign multiple characters to the letters

---

because the number of trigrams give 22^3 (to the power 3) = 10,648 arrangements for which the three digits would not be sufficient.

and syllables which are repeated more than once, in order to diversify them, not to keep the natural arrangement of numbers, and finally to observe that all has been proposed in a separate treatise, where the method of the cipher tables and how to use them for indecipherable text, and use all the observations that are constantly laid down in various places of this book and that there is no better judge than the quality of the encryption that can be intercepted and strives to a perfect connection between all places, by providing an opportunity to exist."

The deciphering treatise that we have briefly analysed is a remarkable work for this period.
The author shows an extensive knowledge of the subject; the treaty is a coherent and comprehensive set of data, precepts, and rules. It was not until the second half of the nineteenth century that progress was made in decryption, including double substitution methods. This was the work of Kasinski, Valerio and Bazeries.

The subjects of the material, the clear and rational description of the deciphering systems, the classification of the elements of the deciphering - the frequency of the letters, the characteristics of the Spanish and French languages - as well as the method followed in the decipherment of the dispatches proposed, place this work above remarkable works, extremely rare indeed of that time.
It remains superior to other more modern works.

At the end of this book, the author refers to another treatise which constitutes an application of the theories he has set forth.[30] We looked for it in vain at the General Archives of Royaume [31]. We hope that another researcher will discover it one day because the value of this first treatise gives enough reason to suspect the second will be worthwhile as well.

Before finishing the introduction, we would like to express our deep gratitude to the canon Mr. R. Aubert, and for the interest he showed in the publication of this work, as well as to Mr. B. Van den Eynde who committed to collect and transcribe the cryptographic texts.

---

[30] See page 68
[31] Archives Générales du Royaume. (DS)

J. DEVOS

Treatise on the art of decryption [32]

The art of deciphering [33] is certainly one of the most difficult that there is in the world, since it works on principles that are fortunately not always at the hands of those who would like to use it, as is recognized by the limited amount of people that has seen and used it.

It is easier to learn something that is entirely unknown than that of we already know, it is sufficient to use simple reasoning and use the workings of syllogism [34], but wanting to penetrate something unknown by somebody who is no less educated and developed and has the true thought of man, through the clouds that cover him and in the middle of unknown characters, it is doing more than all the philosophers together and that is to say, to derive something from nothing.

All the sciences and all the arts have distinct principles from which we draw the conclusions that relate to them.

All the sciences and all the arts have distinct principles from which we draw the conclusions that relate to them.

Astrology itself offers us small aspects, with all mysterious inside it, gives out its predictions (1vo) and the situations on stars, the motions, and revolutions, which are things known to them and authorized by experience. Physics only reasons on effects that our senses perceive every day, which form a chain and have a regular order, and which are always the same when the same causes concur in it, since it is constant that nature always acts in perfect uniformity.

Medicine applies and keeps its prescriptions at certain maxims that have been universally accepted and have their certainty grounded in reasoning and even during the experience of several centuries and before reducing them to practice on a particular subject, she observes the movement of the pulses; the temperament of the person, the signs of illness, which embarrass even the most skilful, provided that they are equivocal [35], that is to say, if they are far from this

---

[32] ARCHIVES GÉNÉRALES DU ROYAUME (Bruxelles), Secretaria de Estado y de Guerra, n° 3.
[33] I will both use the words decryption and deciphering (DS)
[34] A syllogism uses logical arguments and deductive reasoning (DS)
[35] open to more than one interpretation; ambiguous (DS)

certainty and this fixed point, that must regulate all our judgments and direct all our vows in the application of every science.

Theology establishes its assurance in that of the revelation and the guarantee it has in the truth of God itself. Jurisprudence has its own laws and customs, and since they are for most part dependent on authority, it is however very constant that they are founded in reason, which is always the same, that it can't be altered by private individuals, and there is a ray of natural light which is altered by private individuals, and that there is a ray of natural light that changes by the peculiar,
and there is a ray of natural light which enlightens us the least use of the principles of this science.

Geometry has its point, its line, its area, its figure, its centre, its circumference, its problems, and its theorems which are all indisputable things either by evidence of their own or by force of reasoning in their most abstract speculations. It is not known to all that geometry has no guarantee in some of the demonstrations which form the elements of its science.
The arithmetician has his square roots and cubic roots, his propositions, and his relations of numbers, which are very assured things and can't mislead in all the different combinations of the so-called discrete quantity.

Finally, there is no science, no art, which does not know its principle, its first notions and its ideas, some obvious and indisputable, which must direct all its operations.

It is only the art of decryption that seems to have nothing certain, no certainty offered,
to those who offers us something unknown, to come to the knowledge of another,
(2vo) and with simple conjectures and that leads us to a clear and obvious understanding of what we are looking for, but with so many detours and in a journey with little expectations,
that many people say the danger and road to success is of equal importance for those who have walked the path and did succeed.

Because the cipher depends on the imagination of an individual who can use character for which he wants to signify a letter, a syllable, a word and even a whole sentence and which can change that meaning whenever it pleases him, it seems that no fixed precept can be given to this matter, and that everything

depends on the imagination of the one who makes up the number. And on the
satisfaction of his correspondent, who is willing to concur with him and come to
an agreement, that a certain marking or character will mean a certain thing,
what one calls in school: 'signum ex instituto'. [36]
It is not in the power of men to change the meaning of natural signs; an
astrologer or a physicist can't make this or that, or wind or rain or not; he must
stick to what the order of nature decides.

But in terms of ciphers, he who's in the power of the most whimsical writing,
regulates the meaning of things according to the various ideas of his caprice. He
can decide today that 24 means heaven and tomorrow he could want it to mean
the earth, so whoever wants to decipher can say at the beginning the application
that it will plunge into this chaos of poets where there is no order, no light.
He does not know if such a character represents an A. or a B. or a C. or some
other letter of the alphabet, if it is a syllable or a word or a null; he hesitates
always, he doubts everything, and nothing is certain that is under his
investigation.

It is told that Archimedes once used the globe of the earth like a ball to play with
in his hand and if he were given a fixed point on the globe, he could place there
his foot. Our decipherer does a lot more, and without having a fixed point, he
scents and scans the thoughts of men so well, how hidden these might be, and
he will penetrate the mystery despite all the disguises. And at first it seems that
there is nothing very certain and it all depends purely on the phantasy of
somebody else, and consequently no one can be assured of this art.
(3vo)
I hope however, that the experience will show the opposite and that on the
knowledge of the
matter, there is nothing impossible by our intellect, when it is supported by a
strong application.

We will first give in this treatise the general principles of decipherment, then we
will deduce the particular principles, which will be developed in more detail the
mysteries of this art;
after which we will come to the application of these general and axioms, by
giving the assured method of deciphering the simple ciphers in French and
Spanish and then the composite ciphers, syllables and words which are used by

---

[36] The significance of the character is set by the inventor (DS)

all the secretaries in Europe, and we will carefully check the rules and axioms of this method by proposed examples.

And since there are certain ways to cipher by square tables, triangular or other figures that at first seem to be very ugly, we will establish an infallible method to overcome them. And finally, we will deal with indecipherable ciphers with which we will finish this work whose imperfections seem to deserve all the more attention for him that commits himself to walk the path, that he has opened himself and enters a road that he does not yet believe that has been opened for anyone.

Chapter I : General principles on the art of decryption

The cipher is nothing else than speaking in academic terms, then a third significance by which the thoughts of men are regulated and coordinated between two or more persons who communicate their sentiments and disguise themselves to all those who are not from the ministry.
I say third significance because the first sign of man's thoughts is the word by which we explain to others what is known only to ourselves.

The second significance is the written word, which is the sign of the word, and thus a mediator between de thought and the third is the cipher that is the direct sign of the written word, and consequently a second sign of the word and a third sign of thought, a way of which one directly knows the thoughts of God, at which point there would be no existence for the art of decryption, since it is very certain that when one knows the thing signified, one no longer needs a sign.

Whence it follows that the angels can't properly use numbers between themselves; since they know each other's thoughts in God immediately, (4vo) or at least the direction of those thoughts, and those don't suffer the same disguise problems that speech is capable of.

It is not that they can't agree among themselves, when they have certain thoughts, their intention would behave opposite when getting the knowledge from others and their true feelings, in which case it might be said that their real thoughts are the true ciphers, but since they are also a sort of lie, it is not believed that spirits use disguises themselves because they are united into a sovereign truth.

From the definition I have just given of the ciphers in the sense used in this treatise, it seems at first that one could draw therefore that it must also be difficult to decipher a letter for someone that does not have the key,
that it would be like a European to explain a letter written in the Chinese language without knowing it, nor to have a dictionary or interpreter of the language of China, which is now not an unknown signal of thought of a man from that country anymore, cause the cipher is an unknown signal from an individual in written words and are from unknown thoughts towards another party.

And yet one can give general principles to make an Art for this decryption. First it must be supposed that although speech is the signal of thought, it is nonetheless very constant and it's more limited than thought, that one can make more different thoughts than one can invent words to express them.

The reason for this explanation is that thoughts do not only depend on the soul, which is all spiritual, it can act more universally than the body, and can create as many thoughts as there are things present or possible, and for all the different actions for all things, cause thoughts are nothing else than present applications on intentional ideas that we have on these things or on actions.

Instead of the words depending on the body, which is determined by certain limited actions by organs which are there, they can't transcend the limited power of the cause which produces it. (5vo) In effect, words are nothing else than that what is given by their natural being, certain movements of organs, such as the tongue, lips, teeth, and other parts which serve the purpose of speaking, and these motions can't be diversified so much that they can match the number of the ideas that the soul can be create, it follows from this that there will never be a man, who can invent as many different words, as he can have thoughts, and it is from this that equivocations of the same word arise, which sometimes signifies various things and the descriptions and we are often obliged to use words in another language when we need specific particular terms.

To this supposition, which is obvious, is added another which is not less important, and I say that if words are more limited than thoughts, the syllables that compose words are much more limited than they, since they are only the combinations inside them, and that there is no doubt that the number of things that can be combined together is much less than the number of combinations that can be made of those, and we see a familiar example of this in music, which is composed of only a few different tones, but provides us with so many different arts that every day we can find some and discovers new ones.

There are only five primitive colours: white, black, red, green, yellow and yet we could say that there are only the first two, and the other three are composed of these first two, being certain that for white to become black we must go through all other colours in between, it is necessarily to understand all the possible colours and yet there is such a enormous quantity of different colours, which could be a thousand different shades for green; in fact, there is not a leaf on every kind of tree, not a foot of every kind of grass, which has a green colour perfectly similar to that of another species.

The simple ciphers with units up to ten (excluded), are only nine in number, and yet combined together where they have only once a nine, they have ninety different combinations (90), three digits make eight hundred ninety and nine (899) [37], and four digits make eight thousand nine hundred ninety and nine (8999), and the nine digits being combined together by the number of nine (999.999.999) produce eight hundred and seven thousand and six million five hundred and forty-three thousand two hundred and ten combinations (876.543.210) [38] , so one now it easily convinced that by taking the number 123456789, one can that number before coming to 999.999.999, and that at each addition it is necessary that the value of the number of a single unit, and their combination of the digits, change.

We can now conclude that the words, being only the combinations of syllables, it is necessary that they exceed the number 10 and that for the same reason, there are many more syllables than there are simple characters, and the syllables consist only of letter combinations.

In fact, for a very big amount of words that are used in each language, there are only a 100 syllables and 70 inverted of each two letters and about 1170 of each three letters, and for all the syllables there are only 24 letters of different characters in the alphabet, but no more than 30 thirty letters in other languages, because these are all the sounds than humans can articulate and can make. For most nations there are 24 characters, of which the major ones, which are the liaisons to other letters, are known under the name of the 5 vowels. These are the basic essence of the language and without the help of these 5 vowels one can't make a syllable.

The way that the great multitude of words is used on commerce, the decipherer must only limit himself to apply the known principles on which the combinations are composed, that the same principles apply to all different words.

Thirdly, I suppose that, as each nation has its own language, it also affects certain letters which are more used than others, because the French language

------

[37] We are talking about permutations here. When we have two digits using the digits 0…9, and the range is 10…99 (included), we would have 90 permutations. Using three digits would give 900 permutations between 100…999 (included). Having 899 permutations would assume that we start at 101 for example, because there is one short. (DS)
[38] Indeed 999999999-123456789=876.543.210 (DS)

very often uses the letter E., the Italian the letter I., the Spanish the letter O. and
in Latin the letter U. and almost all have this in common, they very often use the
letter S.
It would be unwise to say why, except that as we usually tend to use the easiest
words in a language and the sound S seems to have a nice ring to us than other
consonants and we will use it more regularly.

That the French uses the letter E. more often than any other vowel, the Italians
the letter I. and the Spanish the letter O., may be because these nations have
very different moods; the one has the gentleness and the fluidity, the other the
playfulness and another the seriousness.
Besides that, the vowels have certain cleanness and express a certain passion; as
we all know the E. pronunciation is much softer and more fluid than other
vowels. The letter I is strong and playful and is closest to laughter of a person
and the O. is very heavy but very clean for use in seriousness. (7vo)

If it is the true reason or not, it has always been constant the case, and leaves no
place to doubt it, that also the guttural letters [39] are more common to the
northern nations than to the others, because they are overweight, and the
organs of the voice are coarser, more filled, and therefore more suitable to
pronounce these kinds of letters.

From all that is said above, we must draw the conclusion that when we know the
language type, we know a little bit what letters and syllables are associated with
it. Then it is all easier to approach the knowledge of the cipher that express them
because of their frequent repetition, which must correspond to that of the letter
or syllable they signify.

These are the general principles of decryption that can be used to reduce it into
a few words, because all languages are composed only of a limited number of
words, and words of a limited number of syllables, and the syllables of a much
smaller number of letters. And among them there are several which are rarely
used, and consequently very little used very often. It follows that the
cryptographer needs only to start working at a very small number of characters
which are those, that he notices to be most often repeated, and the discovery
infallibly leads him to the knowledge of the others, which will be explained here
in more detail.

---

[39] The word guttural literally means 'of the throat' and was first used by phoneticians to
describe the Hebrew glottal letters Aleph, Hey, Chet, Ayin and Resh. (DS)

26

Chapter II: Specific principles on the art of decryption

Since there are so many ways of encryption and the rules for decryption are divers, don't be embarrassed in the investigation of them. The first care that must be taken in decryption is to recognize whether the cipher uses a simple key or is composite, if it is regular or irregular, encrypted with specific things and finally in which language is the letter that is in your hands.

This last circumstance is easily recognized, either by clear words which sometimes intersperse the cipher, or by the superscription of the date, by the signature, or by the quality of the persons who wrote it. I call a simple cipher the one that uses only the letters of the alphabet, and a composite cipher contains the letters, syllables, half words, and the whole words, such as are usually used in the Secretaries. (8vo)

The <u>regular cipher</u> is one in which the characters always express the same things and <u>irregular cipher</u> where they change their meaning vary for all the various places where it occurs.
The <u>simple cipher</u> is recognized first of all by the few diversities of the characters of which it is composed, which never exceed the number of twenty-five or thirty, and it is the easiest to decipher. The <u>composite cipher</u> is distinguished by the big variety of its characters, which are into hundred, two hundred, and sometimes as much as five or six hundred, and it requires more research and labour to be decrypt.

We know that the cipher is *irregular* when we see that a same character is repeated by more than three or four times, without the blemish of any other character, as if there were in a numerical cipher we have the following 12 15 26 26 26 26 26, it would be an obvious proof that 26 could not always mean the same thing, since we do not see that in any language the same letter or the same syllable can be followed immediately more than four times. Again, this happens very rarely.

The same is true when we see that several numbers are iterated more than two times one after the other, as we see in 44 44 44 35 35 35 etc. it would be a specific clue to an *irregular* cipher; because we have just said it is easy to judge when the cipher is irregular.

One can also see when it is encrypted with a lot of changes when we do not notice any weakness in the whole fabric of the letter, that there is no iterated number many times more than the others and there is no place where the same number is closely followed by something and where one has noticed it meets the same word several times.

After we recognized the cipher by the rules that we have just given, we know how the letter is composed that we have in our hand and in what language it is written, we arrive at the operations of deciphering.

First thing is to arrange all different characters in columns on a piece of paper.[40] The characters or syllables that can be found in the ciphered letter, and arrange them so that the characters are placed according to their natural order and the syllables according to their alphabetical order and draw a line next to each of them, and mark how many times each is repeated in the letter, so we know the proportions between both and the strength of each character.

```
45   + + + + + + + + + + + + + + + + + + + + -           20
46   + + + + + + + + + + + + + + - - - - - - -           14
47   + + + + + + + + + + - - - - - - - - - - -           10
18   + + + + + + + + - - - - - - - - - - - - -            8
49   + + + + + + + + + - - - - - - - - - - - -            9
50   + + + + + + + + + + - - - - - - - - - - -           10
                                          -
ba   + + + + + + + + - - - - - - - - - - - - -            8
be   + + + + + + - - - - - - - - - - - - - - -            6
bi   + + + + + - - - - - - - - - - - - - - - -            5
bo   + + + + + + + + + + + + - - - - - - - - -           12
bu   + + + + - - - - - - - - - - - - - - - - -            4
```

(9vo)

I call the strength of a character, the quantity of its repetitions and the proportion ratio of that quantity to that of another, for example if the number 45 is repeated twenty times in a letter and the number 50 only ten times, then the strength of the first is twenty and ten for the second, and their proportion is respectively double or less than double, and so on of the others. [41]

---

[40] In our modern times we now call this 'letter frequency analysis' (DS)
[41] Measuring their proportion by percentage of the total is convenient and easy: If the Total = 20+10=30. Then the % of the first is 20/30*100%=67% and for the second 10/30*100=33%. (DS)

28

When we know the strength of each character, we must focus on the five or six most important those who have greater strength than the others. Notice the proportions they have between them, and examine them with much attention, dedication, and diligence in all the places where they occur and meet. Do not end the search before you recognized their true meaning or at least that of one of them.

This may be done by the method which will be explained more in the following chapters, were we will deal with each particular cipher specifically and the meaning of these main characters or even that of only one being known, one will have the knowledge of the others, and will have no difficulty there except in the discovery of the first cipher, which begins to unfold now, which is the first fixed object, on which the rest of the decryption will be unveiled.

Before starting to apply the rules and method we just talked about, it is good to say a word or two about the method to discover null markings [42], these can be recognized at the beginning and at the end of words in ciphered letters, since the nulls are there only for amusement and have no real value.

Now the nulls will reveal themselves either by the juxtaposition [43] of their characters (which happens when the tables of the ciphers were not filled with art) or by their specific situation in the ciphered letter. It is to be noticed that usually the officials who encrypt put the nulls at the beginning and at the end of the words or mix them with significant characters in the first and last line only, without applying them to use in the following piece of the text, if not very rarely, to shorten their work, because it's only natural that they save as much trouble as possible.

From which it follows that when one finds certain characters very rarely inside letters but
very often repeated in the first and last lines of words or in places where other letters or numbers (10vo) followed them closely, or else, in places where other characters follow each other too closely.
The purpose of these nulls is to avoid the discovery of dangerous words, as it's a mark that is used in places that we call critical places, the nulls. The significant

---

[42] From now on we will call these dummy characters, *nulls. (DS)*
[43] It is not clear to me how the nulls are side by side, other than that their total count could be the same, or their position in the syllables are somewhat the same (DS)

characters are usually more scattered throughout the ciphered letter by the necessity of using them and the null characters are applied only by choice of the person that encrypts, and from that follows that he applies them to gets the strongest encryption possible.

One can recognize nulls also when they have been used by the encryptor and he did not understand that when having a large number of characters, and he does add a null to every one of them, it will contribute to the decipherment where the slightest negligence can give a lot of grip to the deciphering man.

These are the usual ways of discovering nulls, but if we fail at first, it is not advisable to start their search again from the beginning and it is better to investigate the significant characters whose discovery leads ineffably to that of the nulls. In the contrary of that, knowing the nulls does not always produce full knowledge of the meaning of the significant characters.

Chapter III: Decryption method for simple Spanish and French cipher

When we recognize in the preceding chapter the given rules on that the cipher we want to decrypt, it is a *simple cipher*, which contains only the alphabet without a mix of syllables, and we also know in what language the letter is written, it is very easy to go forward on it.

First set up a table as explained before with the different strength of each character and their proportions. Then the following axioms and rules can be applied to the complete operation and the problems and in the manner that will be presented in this treatise.

1st Axiom
As the alphabet of almost all languages is composed of 22, 23 or at most 24 letters and that among them there are five which serve (11vo) as liaison to others, that one can't form a single syllable without the help of one of them, which for this reason are called vowels as to suggest that their use is to articulate the voice and make it complete.

From that follows that their strength is much greater than that of all the other letters, except for the consonants N.R.S. and sometimes even the letter L. In the Spanish and French language, the consonants N.R.S.F., have a strength often equal to the vowels and sometimes even more,
particularly if I. and U. are involved in the Spanish language and I. and O. in the French language.
These often give way to letters S.R.N. and sometimes to other consonants; but when we know the three main vowels in each language, or only one of them, we soon will know those that remain.

2nd Axiom
In the Spanish language among the vowels the one that predominates is usually the letter A. because all female words have this termination, that there are many words that begin with [a.] or [ad.] and that the same A. is often used alone as article [44] or preposition.
The vowel that follows it in power is the common O. to cause all male and neuter articles do have this plural ending and also used in all verbs in the past tense.

---

[44] Some articles in Spanish are: el.la.lo.los.las.un.una.unos.unas (DS)

It is not that E. does not compete often and even sometimes surpasses the strength of Q. because most of the syllables have this vowel in their middle, as well as the particle [que] and article [de], the pronouns [me][se] etc., but the three vowels A.E.O. are constant there in the Spanish language, then the vowel I. and U. which is usually the least in strength.

3rd Axiom
Among the consonants in the Spanish language, S. never fails to surpass the power of all others, then R. follows, N. goes after that and finally L., which sometimes is equal N. in strength. But these four are undoubtedly the main ones, C.M.D.F. they follow them in strength, though they are rather far back and close together among themselves. But it does not matter to know what those are, and even less concerning are those in the remainder of the alphabet, because once knowing the vowels and the four main consonants, the others will not be difficult to discover. (12vo)

4th Axiom
In the French language among the vowels the E. absolutely prevails over all the others, there are almost no words where this vowel is not found and often even more than once; A. and U. are the following in strength, I. and O. are about equal, but less than the other three and the last four are always lower than the first one.

5th Axiom
In the same language, the consonants with the most strength is very often S. or N., or otherwise R. or F., these four letters are in a process of counterbalancing each other according to the knowledge of chance and speech, and these sometimes exceed the vowels, except the E. which always infallibly dominates, especially if the encrypted letter is long and one can say that S.N.R.F. are the key consonants in this language as are E.A.U. and especially E. are the vowels.

6th Axiom
The letters, which are very often joined together In the Spanish language are: la.lo.de.on.as.os.ar.er.en.et . In the French language these are: ns.nt.re. and often es.

7th Axiom
Never more than five consonants can follow each other immediately and rarely more than four, yet it is necessary that two are at the end of a word and the other two before the other, as in "plus grand", but you can see many vowels in

the French language because there are syllables composed of three vowels and the letter U. often holds one consonant as in this example: *"Il fait beau avoir"*. Here are seven vowels that follow each other [45], and such is not in the Spanish language.

These axioms are supposed to be principles that follow experience. It is nothing more than some special rules that must be used well and getting individual knowledge on characters.
As said before, certain Spanish consonants often have a bigger strength than vowels. It is important to know how to distinguish them.

First rule
This rule will be used to detect the vowels that have the most influence of the consonants that have the most strength as for example in the Spanish language: where A. has the most strength of the vowels and S. between the consonants, following the 2nd and 3rd axiom.

It will often happen that one and the other will be equally powerful in a cipher; to distinguish between them, it is necessary to remember what has been said above about the vowels and the connections between the consonants that form syllables with them. Consequently, they must be so mixed that there is usually a vowel between two consonants, because they are there in much bigger numbers. (13vo)

It follows that the characters which most often repeated in between others are of the least strength and which are placed in bigger distance so that they must form the sounds of the syllables, are infallibly the vowels. It is therefore unhealthy to be mistaken and you must distinguish these from all the consonants, even though some of those are equal in strength. The examples of the following chapters may give a better understanding of this rule.

Second rule
To be able to distinguish the vowels from the consonants that are in equal power, it is necessary to notice that the letters S.A.R.E.O. can compete in strength in the Spanish language and the letters A.N.R.S.T.U. in the French language, with the vowel E. which always infallibly surpasses all others in this language.

---

[45] eau avoi (DS)

To distinguish these vowels from consonants, we must first consider that when we see characters, what the character signifies at that position. That is to say that if letter E. is doubled, it immediately is followed by a consonant, especially in the French language where letters N.S.R.L.F. are often doubled.

I mention this because it can happen that the same vowel follows itself, for example a letter A. or E. at the end of a word meets itself, and at the beginning of another and in these words *"armée, pensée"* etc. or the vowel U. in *"ouvrir, couvrir "* etc., but these encounters seem to be more rare than those of the consonants; they must not hinder the establishment of this rule, besides, when they are vowels because they are simply preceded and followed by a certain other characters of which we assumes it signifies a consonant and on a place where the U. is doubled, it must be necessary that the consonant that follows is a R.

This guaranteed method for vowels and consonants is the most reliable and very necessary by means of success in the deciphering of a simple cipher. Coming to the end, I am obligated to give not too many rules, but let's look at another one.

Third rule
When one sees the same character three times repeated, one can say that it is a vowel, because never can the same consonant be tripled except in the German language, and other northern [46]languages. Except for one case in the Spanish language with the double LL.; as we see in this example: *"llano"*, but in all others we can say that it's a vowel and even (14vo) an A. or an E. in the French language. For example: *"Il passa à Anvers, l'armée campée en deça"* etc. In the Spanish language it's almost always an A. : *"Iva à Alcala"* etc.

Fourth rule
When we see a word or the same character being several times between other characters and so disposed that there is always only one character between them, we must not hesitate that this same character repeated several times so close to another is a vowel because if it was a consonant, it could only form a strange sound and moreover this vowel must be habitually an A. or O. in the Spanish language such as: *"camarada, Alcantara, conocido"* etc. and almost

---

[46] The text uses the word: septentrion. Which is the old reference to the Northern regions (DS)

always an E. in the French language for example: "*Je ne me releveray point de cette cheute*" etc.

Fifth rule

To recognize the SS. which are very often used in the Spanish language and to distinguish them from the A. with which they sometimes compete, one must consider their situation, because as usual they meet at the end of words. It is possible to arrive at the true meaning of the characters by their distance as in this example: "*las muchas y grand pruevas que losfieles vassallos de Borgona dieron de su zelo*" etc. The S. at the end of each word can easily be recognized in this situation.

Sixth rule

To discern consonant R. in both Spanish and French, we must consider the character which ordinarily follows it, is a consonant. We may even consider itself as consonant, for it is certain that it can only be an R. that is the only one that can be followed immediately by the consonants br.cr.dr.fr .gr.pr.tr.
It is true that sometimes we find in the same situation bl.fl.gl.pl. but it is easy to differentiate the L. from R. because that it's often arranged in a way that there is only one vowel between two of them.
As can be seen in several infinitives in Spanish and French like: "*obrar, ponderar, discurrir, opérer, recouvrir, découvrir*". Moreover, the letter R. is often found after all the vowels, in such a way that it can be said that it's found indifferently everywhere after the vowels and after the consonants.

Seventh rule

When we notice two characters joined together, in different places of that we suspect to be two vowels and which follow another character which is rarely used, if it is not in this same situation, we can say that it is the particle "*que*", because it is used often in speech and it's the first letter Q., it's rarely found elsewhere without at least being joined to U.
(15vo)

Eight rule

If one sees the same character double, it must be FF., which often can be found in French, "*offrir, affaiblir*" or a LL. in "*elle, citadelle, bagatelle*" and in Spanish, "*lla, ella*" etc. or NN. in French: "*connaitre, honneur*" etc., or P. in "*apprendre*" or SS. in "*puissance*" or TT . "*attribuer*" or U. in "*ouvrir, pouvoir, souvenir*" and sometimes E. as in "*armée, espèce*".

Ninth rule
One can still reflect about the same characters in a certain small distance as in
this word *"tout"*, the letter T. is at the first and fourth place and two different
vowels in between. In the word *"vous"*, and in the word *"elle"* there are two of
the same vowels at either side of the LL.

Tenth rule
When we notice a cipher character which we already think is a vowel, preceded
immediately by another and followed by the same, we can reasonably decide
that this one must be a consonant because a vowel can't be repeated twice, if
not very rarely, and in the connection of several words and this consonant
precedes often and follows a vowel and must be N.R. or S.

Eleventh rule
By the axioms given at the beginning of this chapter and by applying the quoted
rules we can suspect a certain character, or we see specific repetition, for
example A. E O. S. R., one needs to look at the contacts of them individually with
the places where it stands. By reasoning and by using all the rules laid down, one
decides for each character sequentially that it can't be this of that and deduced
from the same rules what it can't be, then finally after having rejected all that it
can't be, come to know what it really is.

This is known as determination by negation, like by comparison one knows God,
by the negation of all that is imperfect and limited in creatures. This is how in
certain operations of algebra we know that out of three things proposed, two
must be equal, before we know the relation of inequality that exists between
things, we must know what the relation between them is, then we also know
what is equal between them. (16vo)

This is the main rule and enables the other ones to be used, and it does not only
serve the decipherment of the simple ciphers but also the composite cipher, as
we will see in later chapters which will deal with those and the usage of syllables
as one of the things we will discuss on the simple letters of the alphabet.

One could ask a question based on the previous rules and composite ciphers,
and ask whether these rules are certain and infallible, and if they really work,
cause when one applies them properly, one can succeed if one adds a little faith
to it. That is the main answer I give usually regarding to this reality question.

For it is certain that one must not add faith a simple truth, but when there are several joined together which compete with a mutual truth, the assembled truth must be true in morality and equally physically, then it is a genuine demonstration.

The same is true of the rules that we use to establish the art of decryption, because the different combinations in a language comes from the variety of thoughts and speech of men, and it is the reason why a specific rule in the art of decryption have been considered in particular not be certain and infallible, because in every ciphered letter the risk exists that there will not be one standard way of making a proper application of the rules.

But all things considered, it is certain that they are infallible, and that he who knows how to use them will never fail to decipher the letters from the Secretaries, as we have experienced in the Netherlands during the entire the first war. And the reason that these rules are assured generally are due to the fact that the person who ciphers an especially long letter especially, does not use ordinary and random numbers, and he is preoccupied with the encryption which exposes him to certain weakness, which can be used by the decipherer happily by applying the proposed rules, or at least some of them, with which he will not fail to intercept the key of the cipher.

Chapter IV: Application of the defined axioms and rules

The method of decryption is a true art, and it would not sufficiently be treated
with accuracy, if at the same time the rules would be proposed without giving
examples of their application. So, I am obliged to propose two in in this chapter.
(17vo) One for the Spanish language and the other for the French language.
Then composed ciphers will be treated where the decryption is more difficult
and much more helpful than that of the simple ciphers: those are not often used
by the Secretaries. Talking about it here has nothing to do with the art of
deciphering, so let us start first with the easiest things.

<u>First problem</u>

Assume that one intercepted a Spanish cipher letter with the following message:

10. 11. 9. 11. 20. 8. 18. 12. 11. 6. 20. 18. 3. 13. 16. 8. 22. 8. 14.
22. 6. 3. 13. 16. 8. 22. 6. 18. 6. 9. 22. 10. 11. 14. 22. 6. 10. 1. 14. 22. 6. 16. 8. 2 2. 10. 19.
18. 6. 22. 6. 4. 22. 12. 9. 11. 19. 11. 6. 13. 10. 7. 5. 18. 6. 18. 9. 22. 12. 11. 6. 14. 22.
16. 11. 8. 12. 22. 1. 12. 22. 10. 18. 8. 22. 19. 11. 10. 7. 5. 18. 6. 18. 15. 22. 10. 20. 18.
8. 18. 19. 11. 10. 11. 19. 18. 8. 1. 20. 13. 6. 4. 13. 10. 17. 5. 13. 8. 5. 10. 22. 6. 20. 18.
11. 4. 8. 22. 6. 14. 22. 6. 14. 18. 4. 8. 22. 6. 7. 5. 18. 14. 14. 22. 12. 22. 10. 5. 11. 19.
22. 14. 18. 6. 1. 19. 11. 10. 6. 11. 10. 22. 10. 4. 18. 6.

We immediately recognize that this is a simple cipher because there are only
twenty different characters. Thereafter we examine the strength of each
character, according to the method as described in the second chapter. And
notice that when we sort these on strength, we see the five or six characters that
are the most powerful in the following image. (18vo)

1	++++ ________________________	4
2	________________________	0
3	++ ________________________	2
4	+++++ ________________________	5
5	++++++ ________________________	6
6	++++++++++++++++++++ ____	20
7	+++ ________________________	3
8	++++++++++++ ____________	12
9	++++ ________________________	4
10	+++++++++++++++ _________	15
11	+++++++++++++++ _________	15
12	++++++ ________________________	6
13	++++++ ________________________	6
14	+++++++++ ________________	9
15	+ ________________________	1
16	++++ ________________________	4
17	+ ________________________	1
18	+++++++++++++++++ ________	17
19	+++++++ ________________	7
20	+++++ ________________________	5
21	________________________	0
22	+++++++++++++++++++++++ _	23

And where sorted, we see the cipher number 22 is counted 23 times, etc.

22	+++++++++++++++++++++++ _	23
6	++++++++++++++++++++ ____	20
18	+++++++++++++++++ ________	17
10	+++++++++++++++ _________	15
11	+++++++++++++++ _________	15
8	++++++++++++ ____________	12
14	+++++++++ ________________	9
19	+++++++ ________________	7

These six characters are those with the highest strength and one has reason to believe according to the first axiom of the third chapter that these are the five vowels A.E.I.O.U. and the consonant S. or at least the three vowels A.E.O. and the three consonants N.R.S.

According to the second axiom we convinced ourselves that the cipher number 22 is A. Because this is the vowel that repeats itself most often in Spanish or it is the letter S. following the third axiom. Because out of all the consonants, that one is used most often, and sometimes, following the first rule of the same chapter, it counterbalances with the principal vowels.

And when we know, by means of the conjecture, which one of these two it is, we will have half proof that 6 (as the character that follows 22 in strength) will be the other one, is 22 is A.
Apparently 6 will be S. or exact the opposite if 22 is S. then 6 will be A. undoubtedly and the main thing is to discern which of the two is the vowel and which is the consonant.

To solve this problem, it is necessary to notice in detail all the places where the 22. is found and where those touch the 6 and apply all the rules that has been given to make an assessment on the 22. in comparison to the 6. is placed between numbers which are repeated the least, except when it is near six that it often precedes and that on the contrary to 6. is placed between the number which are repeated the most, by following the first rule 22. must then be a vowel and therefore A. and 6. is then a consonant and therefore S.

This conjecture is supported by another observation taken from the 5th rule, because the situation of the 6. is such that looking at the distances there is reason to believe that it often is at the end of words, until it sees itself at the very end of the article and therefore it is an S.
Especially because it very often follows the number 22. of which we suspect is the letter A. and it is perfectly in line with the 6th axiom since these two characters would make the 'inverted syllable' [47] as which is often found in the Spanish language.

The 8th rule still supports the same conjecture, because as in the line of the cipher that is the last bust one, there is a double 14. that is followed by a 22. Then 14. must be a consonant and according to all appearances it is the L. ,

---

[47] Metathesis. In this context interesting to mention Verlan, a French street slang language where syllables are reversed to create new words (DS)

following the same rule, that 22. must be a vowel and to be exact the A. by the preceding conjectures, which is confirmed by another remarkable circumstance. Which is that in four places of the ciphered article there 22. precedes 6. where one believes that there is the syllable *"as"*, we also note that the same 22. is preceded by 14. which is L. according to the assumption that we have just made, using the 8th rule, would fit very well with "as" in making "*las*". (19vo)

All these conjectures, which are very naturally produced by most of the rules which have been established in the third chapter, give reason to believe that 22. is A. 6-5 and also 5-4 could be L. , we assume this to be true based on many clues, and it is assumed based on these three numbers 22.6.14. they could stand for the letters A.S.L. and if we no longer doubt this (as is usual in algebraic analysis), they are respectively marked as the same numbers in all the places where they meet.

If these are their true meanings, they shine a new light on the discovery of the other numbers or if the conjectures on which they are based are not true, one can discover the faults by comparing that with the other numbers, and carry out a new research operation between them and look for other resemblances, until one is successful in these conjectures and can make a plan on the copy of the article that shows a primary decryption.

```
                                             s                                     a         l    a    s
10 . 11 .  9 . 11 . 20 .  8 . 18 . 12 . 11 .  6 . 20 . 18 .  3 . 13 . 16 .  8 . 22 .  8 . 14 . 22 .  6 .

                        a    s         s         a              l    a    s                   a    s
 3 . 13 . 16 .  8 . 22 .  6 . 18 .  6 .  9 . 22 . 10 . 11 . 14 . 22 .  6 . 10 .  1 . 14 . 22 .  6 . 16 .

      a                        s    a    s         a                             s                        s
 8 . 22 . 10 . 19 . 18 .  6 . 22 .  6 .  4 . 22 . 12 .  9 . 11 . 19 . 11 .  6 . 13 . 10 .  7 .  5 . 18 .  6 .

           a                   s    l    a                             a                   a
18 .  9 . 22 . 12 . 11 .  6 . 14 . 22 . 16 . 11 .  8 . 12 . 22 .  1 . 12 . 22 . 10 . 18 .  8 . 22 .

                             s              a
19 . 11 . 10 .  7 .  5 . 18 .  6 . 18 . 15 . 22 . 10 . 20 . 18 .  8 . 18 . 19 . 11 . 10 . 11 . 19 .

                        s                                            a    s
18 .  8 .  1 . 20 . 13 .  6 .  4 . 13 . 10 . 17 .  5 . 13 .  8 .  5 . 10 . 22 .  6 . 20 . 18 . 11 .  4 .

      a    s    l    a    s    l                   a    s                   l    l    a         a
 8 . 22 .  6 . 14 . 22 .  6 . 14 . 18 .  4 .  8 . 22 .  6 .  7 .  5 . 18 . 14 . 14 . 22 . 12 . 22 . 10 .

                a    l         s                        s              a                   s
 5 . 11 . 19 . 22 . 14 . 18 .  6 .  1 . 19 . 11 . 10 .  6 . 11 . 10 . 22 . 10 .  4 . 18 .  6 .
```

This primary plan aims at signifying some words (if one may call it this) this skeleton of decryption appears between the lines of the cipher and if we imagine the terms that are in line with them, one can find other characters which happily will lead to the decryption at the end of his work.

But if the assembly of the letters is not yet in a way that it can't produce the order of the letters and the meaning for the space between them, it is necessary to try to find some other characters with the help of the proposed rules and think some more.

Because 22 has the most strength it signifies A. and 6. which follows immediately signifies S. according to the hypothesis. (21vo)

The number 18. which follows the 6. in strength and the first and second axiom must be the O. or E., R. or N., because by the assumptions above it can no longer express A. or S. or L., and it can't either be N. nor R. because I notice that it stands immediately before the 6. which signifies S. at the end of the article, and that I do not know a Spanish text, that ends with "*ns.*" or "*rs.*".
So I conclude by the last rule of this negative reasoning that 18. must be a vowel, and it is not A., because that has already been assigned, and it is not I. or U. because the strength is too great for it and therefore it can be an E. or O.

I also consider all the places where this number 18. is place, to decide which of these two vowels E. or O. it represents, if I do not see any place where it can represent the one or the other, as shown in the proposed example. I change the focus of investigation to another character that will reveal itself to me and perhaps then I will come to a point that will show which of these two vowels it is. Therefore, I look at to the next two numbers which are equal in strength, these are 10. and 11. And since I think I already know A.S.L. and as well the last E. or O., I conjecture that 10. and 11. will mean these last-mentioned ones, which will not be significant to 18. or N. or R. according to the first axiom.

And to clarify it: I observe the place where these two numbers are most often found together, and I notice that it is at the end of the article or where we see the following characters:

<pre>
                s   a   s
  1 . 19 . 11 . 10 . 6 . 11 . 10 . 22 . 10 . 4 . 18 . 6 .
</pre>

 and having considered their situation I reason accordingly.

Since 22, which I suppose means A., is immediately preceded, and followed by the number 10. This can't be a vowel according to the tenth rule, and it must be N.R. or S.

According to the same rule it can't be S. if we have already assigned to the number 6. Therefore, it will be R. or N.

Suppose it is R, it can be mapped in the cipher like this to visualize it:

```
          r    s        r    a    r              s
1 . 19 . 11 . 10 .  6 . 11 . 10 . 22 . 10 .  4 . 18 .  6 .
```

 and continue reasoning in this direction.

If 10. is R. or when it would be N., the 11. must be a vowel otherwise there will be five consonants, and that is the opposite of what is in the tenth rule. So it must be E. or O., since A. is already occupied and I. and U. are not of such strength; so suppose it is E., Following the previous hypotheses we have the following characters:

```
      e    r    s    e    r    a    r              s
1 . 19 . 11 . 10 .  6 . 11 . 10 . 22 . 10 .  4 . 18 .  6 .
```

(21vo) But as one can see, we have only some gibberish and not a Spanish word and the same would be seen when the number 10. would mean N. instead of R. It is necessary to come to the other end of the supposition that it must be N. or O. and furthermore it is not E. because of the incongruity of the gibberish that shows it is necessary that it is O. and by the preceding reasonings which have left an alternative conjecture that left us undecided about the number 18. This number must be E. or O. and presently one knows that 11. must also be E. or O. and can't be E. So, the E. must be 18, and 11. must be O.

Now the following characters can be marked on the cipher in accordance with all these assumptions and as consequence of our reasoning:

```
      o    r    s    o    r    a    r         e    s
1 . 19 . 11 . 10 .  6 . 11 . 10 . 22 . 10 .  4 . 18 .  6 .
```

But we see that this combination is still gibberish and that the assumptions for 22.=A, 6.=S, 18=E, and 11. that must express O. Now we return to the beginning of the error, and we know that the alternative of 10. for which we remained in doubt, whether it was an N. or a R. was wrongly chosen. Instead, we now take not R. but the N. for 10. We then have the following:

<pre>   o   n   s   o   n   a   n   e   s
1 . 19 . 11 . 10 . 6 . 11 . 10 . 22 . 10 . 4 . 18 . 6 .</pre>

and because I believe that this arrangement of letters has the appearance of a good, pronounced word, I have reason to believe in all my conjectures and I hope for a successful operation. I am only interested in finding a meaningful word in Spanish that is close to the combination of letters that we now have.

If I find already one word that's a good sign and proof that I succeeded and also that it pays off and is useful to discover more letters that are less frequent, after having imagined all the words who approach it, there is none that can be perfectly applied (this can happen often, because all the words of a language are not always present in the mind) we must not be turned off by that, but use other means to come to the verification of all conjectures.

There are many ways, and these must be assumed all true so we can use these in the analysis of the problems of geometry and algebra and therefore we believe in the proposed example that 22. means A., 6-S., 18-E., 11-O., 10-N.

(22vo) Of the ten most powerful numbers which we has chosen previously in the research, there now only remains the 8. for which we must take R., since we know already the three principal vowels, and two of the principal consonants which are N. S., and since R. competes with N. and often surpasses them, according to the previously proposed axioms.

And even when we do not want to make this assumption about R., the truth will reveal itself in the following operation, which gives us the means for the verification of the ways towards the hypotheses that have been made for this problem.

One needs to mark all numbers of which one believes that have been discovered, on the lines of the ciphered article, in the following way:

n   o   o   e   o   s   e   a   i   a   s
10 . 11 . 9 . 11 . 20 . 8 . 18 . 12 . 11 . 6 . 20 . 18 . 3 . 13 . 16 . 8 . 22 . 8 . 14 . 22 . 6 .

                  a   s   e   s   a   n   o   i   a   s   n   i   a   s
3 . 13 . 16 . 8 . 22 . 6 . 18 . 6 . 9 . 22 . 10 . 11 . 14 . 22 . 6 . 10 . 1 . 14 . 22 . 6 . 16 .

    a   n   e   s   a   s   a   o   o   s   n   e
8 . 22 . 10 . 19 . 18 . 6 . 22 . 6 . 4 . 22 . 12 . 9 . 11 . 19 . 11 . 6 . 13 . 10 . 7 . 5 . 18 .

s   e   a   o   s   i   a   o   a   a   n   e
6 . 18 . 9 . 22 . 12 . 11 . 6 . 14 . 22 . 16 . 11 . 8 . 12 . 22 . 1 . 12 . 22 . 10 . 18 . 8 .

a   o   n   e   s   e   a   n   e   e   o   n   o
22 . 19 . 11 . 10 . 7 . 5 . 18 . 6 . 18 . 15 . 22 . 10 . 20 . 18 . 8 . 18 . 19 . 11 . 10 . 11 . 19 .

e   s   n   n   a   s   e   o
18 . 8 . 1 . 20 . 13 . 6 . 4 . 13 . 10 . 17 . 5 . 13 . 8 . 5 . 10 . 22 . 6 . 20 . 18 . 11 . 4 .

    a   s   i   a   s   i   e   a   s   e   i   i   a   a   n
8 . 22 . 6 . 14 . 22 . 6 . 14 . 18 . 4 . 8 . 22 . 6 . 7 . 5 . 18 . 14 . 14 . 22 . 12 . 22 . 10 .

    o   a   i   e   s   o   n   s   o   n   a   n   e   s
5 . 11 . 19 . 22 . 14 . 18 . 6 . 1 . 19 . 11 . 10 . 6 . 11 . 10 . 22 . 10 . 4 . 18 . 6 .

As I see in this scheme most of the vowels and main consonants are very mixed so they form syllables, which confirms my thoughts that I am in the right path and that my assumptions could be true. Now I look for one or more places where I can easily form words and I find in the second line:

e   s   a   n   o   i   a   s
18 . 6 . 9 . 22 . 10 . 11 . 14 . 22 . 6 .

There in the middle of the line these characters can be seen, and we only have to add one more character.

I can form this word *"espanolas"* which I know, and that 9. is a P. The other place is at the beginning of the penultimate[48] line, where these characters are marked:

i   a   s   i   e   a   s
14 . 22 . 6 . 14 . 18 . 4 . 8 . 22 . 6 .

---

[48] second one from the end

This gives reason to believe that, by their combination, that these words *"las letras"* can be seen here, especially according to the remark made previously on this big subject, it is important to suspect that 8. means R. which is confirmed by the observations of the 6th rule of the previous chapter, which are all valid with respect to the number 8. in this problem.

Cause it is often seen after different characters where one must decide between consonants such as 20. 16. 4. and equally after the vowels and sometimes also after or before the same vowel, which all are observations of the 6th rule.

And this way we know three new letters in the two places that we just noticed that we recognize as P. R. F. We must be smart here in the verification of those that remained to be guessed, so we can add them to the others that are already marked on the scheme:

```
 n    o    p    o         r    e         o    s         e                   r    a    r    l    a    s
10 . 11 .  9 . 11 . 20 .  8 . 18 . 12 . 11 .  6 . 20 . 18 .  3 . 13 . 16 .  8 . 22 .  8 . 14 . 22 .  6 .

                r    a    s    e    s    p    a    n    o    l    a    s    n         l    a    s
 3 . 13 . 16 .  8 . 22 .  6 . 18 .  6 .  9 . 22 . 10 . 11 . 14 . 22 .  6 . 10 .  1 . 14 . 22 .  6 . 16 .

 r    a    n         e    s    a    s    t    a         p    o         o    s         n              e
 8 . 22 . 10 . 19 . 18 .  6 . 22 .  6 .  4 . 22 . 12 .  9 . 11 . 19 . 11 .  6 . 13 . 10 .  7 .  5 . 18 .

 s    e    p    a         o    s    l    a         o    r         a         a    n    e    r    a
 6 . 18 .  9 . 22 . 12 . 11 .  6 . 14 . 22 . 16 . 11 .  8 . 12 . 22 .  1 . 12 . 22 . 10 . 18 .  8 . 22 .

      o    n         e    s    e         a    n         e    r    e         o    n    o
19 . 11 . 10 .  7 .  5 . 18 .  6 . 18 . 15 . 22 . 10 . 20 . 18 .  8 . 18 . 19 . 11 . 10 . 11 . 19 .

 e    r              s    t    n              r         n    a    s         e    o    t
18 .  8 .  1 . 20 . 13 .  6 .  4 . 13 . 10 . 17 .  5 . 13 .  8 .  5 . 10 . 22 .  6 . 20 . 18 . 11 .  4 .

 r    a    s    l    a    s    l    e    t    r    a    s              e    l    l    a         a    n
 8 . 22 .  6 . 14 . 22 .  6 . 14 . 18 .  4 .  8 . 22 .  6 .  7 .  5 . 18 . 14 . 14 . 22 . 12 . 22 . 10 .

      o         a    l    e    s              o    n    s    o    n    a    n    t    e    s
 5 . 11 . 19 . 22 . 14 . 18 .  6 .  1 . 19 . 11 . 10 .  6 . 11 . 10 . 22 . 10 .  4 . 18 .  6 .
```

This scheme is arranged and composed such a way that the letters of which we know the individual combination are shown, and those that are unknown and are less frequent like C.U.I.M.D.Q. can be found easily.

No podremos decifrar las cifras espanolas ny las francesas tampoco, sin que sepamos la forma y manera con que se han de reconocer y distinguir unas de otras las letras que llaman vocales y consonants.

<u>COROLLARY</u>

From this problem it may be inferred that:

1) the main thing in the art of deciphering is to know how to doubt well and how to conjecture, in accordance with the rules and axioms which have been established in the preceding chapters, and that doubts of this nature driven by art and by method, can only end when one has certain knowledge and proof

2) the logical negation[49] is very good for discovering unknown characters, since supposing that a number must be something, that the negation is very good for discovering unknown characters. Once a cipher has been formed, assigning a certain letter or another in the beginning, we know it can't be both, and it is obvious that we know which one it really is and we recognize what it can't be. This shows that it's enough to see it signifies one thing, and it is not another thing, and such a character could signify several likelihoods, which are not invalid through the places where they occur, which is based on the principle of metaphysics and morality. *Bonum ex integra causa, malum autem ex quolibet defectu.*[50] (24vo)

3) that if the first conjectures by which it was assumed, according to the rules, that 22. signifies A., 6-S, 14-L., 18-E., 10-N., 11-O., the words could not have been formed, or the less significant words, it must be noticed that the primary assumptions were not correct, and it was necessary to proceed with a new process, in order to form new conjectures that were near to those that we used before, in such a way that from the strength of the numbers and the letters in the alphabet that are represented in the ciphered letters, using the rules and the axioms. And do never get tired or discouraged in your work when you can't find a fixed point of true meaning during the research from which one can't escape. Provided that one has the patience to apply successively these rules on all places of the ciphered text, where we notice weakness and where we believe can be

---

[49] A logical negation is an operation when a proposition produces a value of true when its operand is false and a value of false when its operand is true. See f.e. wikiversity (DS)
[50] Good comes from a whole thing, whereas evil arises from each of the (separate) defects. (DS)

revealed that what is hidden. Based on these rules, they will, all together, never fail.

Second problem

Decryption of a simple cipher in the French language. Suppose we want to decipher the following cipher text:

```
a. 9. L. n. 5. 3. 5. 3. p. d. c. 3. L. a. 3. 4. 2. 3. c. 4. 3. 3. 4. 5. 3. 4.
f. e. 1. 1. 3. 4. 5. 3. m. p. d. 4. 3. 3. 4. 2. 9. L. 5. 3. 4. q. 9. L. 9. q.
n. 3. L. 3. 4. d. c. q. e. c. c. p. 4. c. 3. 4. n. 2. 9. 4. a. c. p. p. L. 9. m. 3.
5. 3. n. e. p. n. a. 3. 1. e. c. 5. 3. 3. n. 2. e. p. L. 8. L. 3. p. 4. 4. d. L.
d. a. o. 9. p. n. 7. 3. 9. p. q. e. p. 2. 5. 3. n. 3. 1. 2. 4. 7. 3. 9. p. q. e.
p. 2. 5. 9. 2. 2. a. d. q. 9. n. d. e. c. 3. n. 4. p. L. n. e. p. n. p. c. 3. 3.
6. n. L. 3. 1. 3. 2. 9. n. d. 3. c. q. 3.
```

This displayed ciphertext [51] contains some errors, these are marked, but since the explanation is based on that, this cannot be omitted, without changing the entire text on it. The correct ciphertext is as follows (DS):

```
a. 9. L. n. 5. 3. 5. 3. p. d. c. 3. L. a. 3. 4. 2. 3. c. 4. 3. 3. 4. 5. 3. 4.
f. e. s. s. 3. 4. 5. 3. m. p. d. 4. 3. 3. 4. 2. 9. L. 5. 3. 4. q. 9. L. 9. q.
n. 3. L. 3. 4. d. c. q. e. c. c. p. 4. c. 3. 4. n. 2. 9. 4. a. e. p. p. L. 9. m. 3.
5. 3. n. e. p. n. a. 3. s. e. c. 5. 3. 3. n. 2. e. p. L. 8. L. 3. p. 4. 4. d. L.
d. a. c. 9. p. n. 7. 3. 9. p. q. e. p. 2. 5. 3. n. 3. s. 2. 4. 7. 3. 9. p. q. e.
p. 2. 5. 9. 2. 2. a. d. q. 9. n. d. e. c. 3. n. 4. p. L. n. e. p. n. p. c. 3. 3.
6. n. L. 3. 5. 3. 2. 9. n. d. 3. c. q. 3.
```

To make it possible to distinguish the number one and the letter 'l', it was necessary to print the L. in capital letters.

It is also necessary, as in the case of the Spanish cipher, to begin with the operation of knowing the different strengths of each character and to mark in the following ways how many times each one is repeated in the cipher.

---

[51] The original ciphertext contained some errors and this the table is not correct, but it is an exact copy from the book. For example, the o. does not occur in the corrected text, and all the 1.'s are wrong. However, for solving a cipher and understanding the method here those small differences do not play a role. (DS)

1	+++++	5
2	++++++++++	10
3	+++++++++++++++++++++++++++++++++	33
4	++++++++++++++++	16
5	+++++++++	9
6	+	1
7	++	2
8	+	1
9	+++++++++++	11
a	++++++	6
c	++++++++++	10
d	++++++++	8
e	++++++++++	10
f	+	1
h		0
L	+++++++++++	11
m	++	2
n	++++++++++++++	14
o	+	1
p	++++++++++++++++	16
q	+++++++	7
r		0

The characters with the most strength are: 3. repeated thirty three times, 4. repeated sixteen times, p. sixteen times, n. fourteen times, 9. eleven times, L. also eleven times, the next three are repeated ten times each, C. has 2.   (25vo)

3	+++++++++++++++++++++++++++++++++	33
4	++++++++++++++++	16
p	++++++++++++++++	16
n	++++++++++++++	14
9	+++++++++++	11
L	+++++++++++	11
2	++++++++++	10
c	++++++++++	10
e	++++++++++	10
5	+++++++++	9

<u>Application of axioms</u>

I follow the application of the axioms and the rules given for the French language and I begin my operation. Since the number 3 is used thirty-three times, half of the size of all others and according to the 4th axiom of the third chapter, this can only be E.
The ones that follow in strength are 4. and P., both equally strong and therefore they can only be A. and U. according to the next rule or according to the same rule or according to the 5th axiom they can be S.N.R. or F.
This needs that on these two equal characters 4 and P. an individual inspection and according to the 11th rule I consider all places of these characters in the cipher and I notice in the 2nd and 3rd lines that the 4. is arranged with the 3. such: 4. 3. 3. 4. On this occasion we use the same eleventh rule to confirm the reasoning that has been assumed.
Since 3. is the E, the number 4. can't be a vowel cause if it was one according to the 4th axiom it would have been the A. or U. or one of these, but there are no words in French that have the vowels "aeea" or "ueeu". Therefore, the number 4. can only be one of the four main consonants reported in the 5th axiom, knowing S.N.R. or F.
But to know precisely which one is represented by which character is not an easy task, cause both fit pretty well in this arrangement, because in the French language at the end of a word is "te" or "ne" is possible and at the beginning a "et" or "en" is also as arrangement of letters and "te, et" or "ne en".
One can also observe this combination "sees" as in these words: "disposées, dispersées," etc. and also this "reer" as in this word "creer" [52]. It is now necessary to take another path to distinguish the things under our investigation, and by using the negative view of which we have spoken often before, come to the positive knowledge of the meaning of the cipher. (26vo)

Therefore, I consider all the numbers which precede and follow a chosen place, the second line where I find that these characters 3. 4. 2. 3. c. 4. 3. 3. 4. 5. 3. 4.
I consider that the 3. means E. according to the axioms and that 4. must be one of the consonants N.R.S.F. Suppose it is N. According to this assumption it would give the following expressions on the place of the number in question:

---

[52] to create (DS)

```
e    n      e        n    e    e    n       e    n
3 . 4 . 2 . 3 . c . 4 . 3 . 3 . 4 . 5 . 3 . 4 .
```

Now we see that there are blank places on hat 2. c. and 5. where we possibly can make whole words. I go through all the letters of the alphabet which are not yet known, and I try to find a known French word, where these characters could fit in and I find that 4. means N. There should be these words: "enberneenten" or "enderneenten" or "enterneenten", etc.

And going through all the letters of the alphabet that I mix with the characters, suppose that I only get gibberish there, then I can assume from this that 3. stands for E. Because it is more probable by the 4th axiom, that the number 4. can't signify N. and hence according to the previous reasonings it must mean R.S. or F.

Next, I perform the same job for R.S.F. where I used the N. before. Going through the alphabet, I find only nonsense about R. and F. But when I come to the S. I find in his favour that it is possible to make words that also makes a half sentence in the French language.

In fact, assuming that 3. means E. and by the negative reasoning I just practically arrived unwillingly at the assumption that 4. means S.   Now, the proposed cipher looks like:

```
e    s      e        s    e    e    s       e    s
3 . 4 . 2 . 3 . c . 4 . 3 . 3 . 4 . 5 . 3 . 4 .
```

By traversing along all the other letters of the alphabet I try to fit anything to places 2. c. and 5.
I see that when I take 2.=p. and c.=n. and 5.=d. Now I can make half a sentence of it:

```
e    s    p    e    n    s    e    e    s    d    e    s
3 . 4 . 2 . 3 . c . 4 . 3 . 3 . 4 . 5 . 3 . 4 .
```

And when I can find another half sentence there (which is not in the example proposed), it would become very easy for the coming operations to find the true meaning, because the truth can only be one (there may be several false and several real appearances on the same subject).
False meanings as one would have assigned a. 2. c. 5. in the wrong half sentence that we got can be recognized as impracticable during the operation, because of the gibberish that they produce in the remainder of the ciphered text. It would always be necessary to return to the last true sense, which is what has been shown by the preceding reasonings. (27vo)

To make this half-sentence a little more complete, we look in the ciphered letter for the character that immediately precedes those which we have just explained, and see if it could be an L, to make something like *"les pensées des"*. And as it can be decided that the letter a. can mean L. because of its mediocre strength, it happens to be like this that we think we already know six characters which are: 3=E., 4=S., 2=p., 0=n., and a=L.

And what confirms all these conjectures is the observation of the 6th axiom, that holds among other remarks, that d. and e. very often follow each other in the French language, as well as E. and S. which is shown in the example of this problem, assumed that the assumptions have been made correctly, as 3 means E., 4-S and 5-d. There the 6th axiom can be applied and can be found in the fabric of the number 4. which very often follows 3. and 3. follows often 5.

All these assumptions have been made by using the axioms and the defined rules, and before we make a new scheme of the cipher, we first write down the characters a. 3. 4. 2. c. 5., the letters are respectively assigned to the meaning of 1.e.s.p.n.d and it follows from that, we now are able to show:

```
  L           d   e   d   e           n   e       L   e   s   p   e   n   s   e   e   s   d   e   s
a . 9 . L . n . 5 . 3 . 5 . 3 . p . d . c . 3 . L . a . 3 . 4 . 2 . 3 . c . 4 . 3 . 3 . 4 . 5 . 3 . 4 .

              e   s   d   e               s   e   e   s   p           d   e   s
f . e . s . s . 3 . 4 . 5 . 3 . m . p . d . 4 . 3 . 3 . 4 . 2 . 9 . L . 5 . 3 . 4 . q . 9 . L . 9 . q .

      e       e   s       n           n   n       s   n   e   s       p       s   L                   e
n . 3 . L . 3 . 4 . d . c . q . e . c . c . p . 4 . c . 3 . 4 . n . 2 . 9 . 4 . a . e . p . p . L . 9 . m . 3 .

  d   e               L   e           n   d   e   e       p                       e       s   s
5 . 3 . n . e . p . n . a . 3 . s . e . c . 5 . 3 . 3 . n . 2 . e . p . L . 8 . L . 3 . p . 4 . 4 . d . L .

      L                       e               p   d   e       e       p   s       e
d . a . c . 9 . p . n . 7 . 3 . 9 . p . q . e . p . 2 . 5 . 3 . n . 3 . s . 2 . 4 . 7 . 3 . 9 . p . q . e .

      p   d       p   p   L                   n   e   p   s                       n   e   e
p . 2 . 5 . 9 . 2 . 2 . a . d . q . 9 . n . d . e . c . 3 . n . 4 . p . L . n . e . p . n . p . c . 3 . 3 .

          e       e   p               e   n       e
6 . n . L . 3 . 5 . 3 . 2 . 9 . n . d . 3 . c . q . 3 .
```

As a result, [53] only the following four main characters must be searched A.U.R.F. between the numbers which are not yet known and which have the greatest strength, that is to say, 9. p. L. n.

It will be needed to knows that these four each represent one of the four letters of the alphabet A.U.R.F. whose verification will be done by application of the established rules and by means of the insights given; in the anatomy of the ciphered character that we just made the half-words are already visible.

---

[53] In the cipher, please notice that the L is displayed as I.

In fact, we must consider only the beginning of the same figure where there are these characters marked: a. 9. L. n. 5. 3. 5. 3. p. d. c. 3. L.

And one reasoned thus that a. is L. and that 9. , which is the next one, must be one of the four letters still unknown in A.U.R.F. and it can't be R. nor F. because L. does not mix well with the other at the beginning of a word, it follows that 9. will mean A. or U., and the cipher L., and n. that follow 9., are also each one of the letters A. U. R. or F. according to the previous assumption.   (28vo)

Now all the combinations that can be given for these four cipher characters

<pre>
              L
          a . 9 . L . n .
</pre>

can only be the following ones: *"luar, luat, lurt, lutr, laur, laut, latr, lart"*, and from these eight combinations, only the last one is significant. It follows that it's the only true one, and consequently of the four principal cipher characters which remains to be known 9.p.L.n. and which must be A. U. R. F., of which we know by this last operation that 9. signifies A, that L. signifies R. and that N. signifies F., and by consequence which necessarily follows from induction we obviously know that p. must mean U. which also matches with its strength being on the third rank.

Placing all these newly discovered four letters, on each of the cipher characters, we will find this half-sentence, at the beginning of the first line:

<pre>
      L   a   r   t   d   e   d   e   u   n   e   r
      a . 9 . L . n . 5 . 3 . 5 . 3 . p . d . c . 3 . L .
</pre>

By which there is reason to believe that d. which is the only cipher char which remains unknown, will signify i. in order to form the words: *"l'art de deviner"*, which is the only possible meaning in this combination.

And immediately after this half sentence we see another which is like this: [54]

---

[54] Here it was noticeable that in previous originals there were some mistakes: the 2nd line the wrong sequence f.e.1.1.3.4. was given. The 3rd line, the a.c.p.p. must be a.e.p.p. 4th line, the a.3.1. must be a.3.s. 5th line, 3.2.1. changed into 3.2.s. and d.a.o.9. into d.a.c.9. Last line, 3.1.3. into 3.5.3. From here all mistakes backwards changed and corrected.

```
L   e   s   p   e   n   s   e   e   s   d   e   s                       e   s
a . 3 . 4 . 2 . 3 . c . 4 . 3 . 3 . 4 . 5 . 3 . 4 . f . e . s . s . 3 . 4 .
```

and since it perfectly follows the first one, we have reason to think that we did not mistake ourselves and the new discoveries that we made through our big insight in this cipher does not entirely cover all characters in the previous. But based on what is already known, it follows that

```
                        e   s
        f . e . s . s . 3 . 4 .
```

can't mean anything else but the word "*hommes*", because on one side it agrees with the half-sense that precedes it to make a complete sentence. And the cipher characters must represent the same letters throughout the cipher, so that for example letters that make a word like *s. s.* perfectly matches *m. m.* on the same places in the word. And finally the power of E. which is worth ten in the strength table corresponds to that of O. and that of the cipher char f. , which is used only once, does not go well with that of h. which is not found very often. We can say that that all these are credible and are a kind of demonstration that proves that these cipher characters express the word which is shown as:

```
h   o   m   m   e   s
f . e . s . s . 3 . 4 .
```

After all these conjectures, plausibility's, reasonings and demonstrations, it is believed that to complete the proposed decipherment for this problem, you work on it the same way if it would have been in the Spanish language. For each character that one takes in the cipher, assume one of the letters of the alphabet, as A. E. I. O. U. d. L. m. n. p. r. s. t. h., and then finally we can get the layout like this one:

(DS)

```
L  a  r  t  d  e  d  e  u  i  n  e  r  L  e  s  p  e  n  s  e  e  s  d  e  s
a. 9. L. n. 5. 3. 5. 3. p. d. c. 3. L. a. 3. 4. 2. 3. c. 4. 3. 3. 4. 5. 3. 4.

h  o  m  m  e  s  d  e     u  i  s  e  e  s  p  a  r  d  e  s     a  r  a
f. e. s. s. 3. 4. 5. 3. m. p. d. 4. 3. 3. 4. 2. 9. L. 5. 3. 4. q. 9. L. 9. q.

t  e  r  e  s  i  n     o  n  n  u  s  n  e  s  t  p  a  s  L  o  u  u  r  a     e
n. 3. L. 3. 4. d. c. q. e. c. c. p. 4. c. 3. 4. n. 2. 9. 4. a. e. p. p. L. 9. m. 3.

d  e  t  o  u  t  L  e  m  o  n  d  e  e  t  p  o  u  r     r  e  u  s  s  i  r
5. 3. n. e. p. n. a. 3. s. e. c. 5. 3. 3. n. 2. e. p. L. 8. L. 3. p. 4. 4. d. L.

i  L     a  u  t     e  a  u     o  u  p  d  e  t  e  m  p  s     e  a  u     o
d. a. c. 9. p. n. 7. 3. 9. p. q. e. p. 2. 5. 3. n. 3. s. 2. 4. 7. 3. 9. p. q. e.

u  p  d  a  p  p  L  i     a  t  i  o  n  e  t  s  u  r  t  o  u  t  u  n  e  e
p. 2. 5. 9. 2. 2. a. d. q. 9. n. d. e. c. 3. n. 4. p. L. n. e. p. n. p. c. 3. 3.

   t  r  e  m  e  p  a  t  i  e  n     e
6. n. L. 3. 5. 3. 2. 9. n. d. 3. c. q. 3.
```

From which we decide the figures m. q. c. 8. 7. 6. that remain to be known, mean the following letters g. c. f. y. b. x. and that the explanation of the whole text is here:

"L'art de deviner les pensées des hommes déguisées par des caractères inconnus n'est pas l'ouvrage de tout le monde et pour y réussir il faut beaucoup de temps, beaucoup d'application et surtout une extrême patience". [55]

<u>COROLLARY</u>

In the first place I can conclude from this problem that in the simple cipher in the French language the vowel E. is always the key and the principle of decipherment since experience shows that its strength incomparably exceeds that of all the other letters. Which is different in the Spanish language, where we have more equality between its main characters, namely A.O.R.S.E..
Which makes the deciphering of Spanish simple ciphers more difficult than that of simple French ciphers.
On the second place, a certain knowledge on plausibility of a specific character is needed, together with many others that can accompany it, and certainty or

---

[55] "The art of guessing the thoughts of men is disguised by unknown characters, is not the work for everyone and in order to succeed, it takes a lot of time, a lot of application, and above all, extreme patience". (DS)

similarities as in a chain reaction, that one pulls out one chain and by it one can define another.

Which makes it very useful to investigate ciphers based on the strength of characters and hold on to that until we know the different characters because on the many places that a character has, it also has connections with others, and that will give us more openings for the decryption of the cipher.

Thirdly. When there are two rules that can be applied to a single character, that seem to contrast with each other, we must always bend to the strongest, even when there is an ambiguity,

and the one that is not, that it must always prevail. I mention a rule ambiguous that can be applied to a character, for example when using the 8thy rule, which is about double characters, it can also be applied to certain consonants or vowels and one can use it when it does not absolutely determine or infallibly defines something.

Now this rule must be corrected by another which is more precise, more definite, and therefore unambiguous, as happens in the example of the proposed problem, where these ciphered characters 4.3.3.4. can be seen. One has reason to believe that by the 8th rule that 3. could be ff. or 11. or nn. or ss. or uu. or even ee. But there is another precise rule which is that the strength of 3. is recognized and must signify E., where one is determined by the other, and the uncertainty of the ambiguous rule is raised by the confrontation of that what is not there.

Fourth. We must finally conclude from all above that the art of deciphering consists only in a pure reasoning of the mind and application supported by the power of the imagination, which at the same time forms several ideas, and represents all reports that a character may or may not have with more than one character in the alphabet.

Either because of their same strength or unequal strength, or by the incompatibility or connection that some letters have with others and consequently the ciphered characters that represent them or the situation in which the numbers finally are placed, gives room for many different conjectures, that the only reasoning must be disproportion, either by the negation or otherwise, to finally reach the object of truth that we are looking for.

Chapter V: Composite ciphers

……. [56] and it must also be that of the person that deciphers that claims he can distinguish between five different meanings and unknown sentences that really represents the alphabetical letter or syllable he is looking for.

To overcome this, it is necessary to observe several things that will be deduced in order, after which we will give examples of decryption of a composite cipher like what we used on the simple ciphers. And for this, we propose two problems, one will be used for the Spanish language and the other for the French language, but we shall start with the following observations that will take the place of axioms and rules.

First observation on the composite ciphers

There are axioms and rules between those that have been defined in the preceding chapters for the discovery of the keys in simple ciphers, which may also be used for the composite ciphers: but there are other rules in between those, and some are useless or even in contrast to what we need to observe and use. These will talk about the differences in languages and the discovery of nulls, the research, and the knowledge of a character by negation … different assumptions; what it does for … this knowledge can also be used in … looking at the simple ciphers and at this … [57]   (31vo)

After all that what has been said about the strength of the vowels and especially E. in the French language and the rules that have been given to distinguish the consonants and to recognize some of them individually, are quite useless for the decryption of the composite ciphers.

And it is often necessary to go in the opposite direction because it is certain for example that the vowel E. is the one with the most strength in a simple cipher in the French language, but in a composite cipher it is one of the characters that has the least strength since the vowel E. is part of all the syllables that have its ending with the letter. It is necessarily compounded with it and this letter is used in words where this vowel forms a specific sound and separates the preceding syllables, like for example these: *"Armée, pensée, connue."*

---

[56] In the original there is here a big empty gap, to the disappearance of a leaflet, which was to be the preamble of Chapter V. Part of the title description is omitted but added by me based on the context. (DS)

[57] In the original, a tear at the bottom of the sheet made the text disappear completely.

In order to avoid confusion with this method, it is necessary to give new rules for the understanding of a composite cipher. There may be ones that are similar like those used for the simple cipher, but we will explain them all in the following observations.

Second observation

In this kind of cipher we do not only look at the strength of the alphabet letters, but primarily to the strength of the syllables, which are there in big numbers, so that instead of five or six characters which we would examine in a simple cipher in order to find the principle for its decipherment, we need to go through a much larger amount of letters and syllables in a composite cipher. In a composed cipher the consonant S. usually surpasses all the other letters and syllables in the table of the cipher, and therefore using the strength table on letters in the Spanish language is only handy for simple ciphers.

But in the tables of the cipher which are regular one has to be cautious that one does not assign several characters to the same consonant, notwithstanding there are means to discover what it stands for, which will be explained further.

Third observation

To give a full explanation of the preceding observation it should be noted that in the composite Spanish cipher, the vowels which have the most power are A. O. the consonants S. R. N. the syllables
co. de. do. la. lo. me. mo. no. que. re. ro. si. ta. to. el. en. on. ar. er. ir. as. es. os. but especially the following ones: *de. do. la. lo. no. que. re.*

And in the French composite cipher the vowels which have the most power are A. U. O. · but especially A. The consonants are N. S. R. F. and the syllables *ce. de. la. le. me. ne. que. re. se. te. en. on. er. is. il. et.* but especially the following ones, that end on E.: *de. le. me. ne. que. re. se. te.*

Fourth observation

The letters and syllables that occur most often in the Spanish language are: co-n. co-mo. la-s. mo-s, ne-s. And those in the French language are: *n-s. n-t. r-t. r-s. de-s. le-s.*

<u>Fifth observation</u>

The letters and syllables which are the most frequent doubled in the French ciphers are A. A. like in
"a avoir, a approcher" etc. F. F. in . *"offrir, affront"* etc. P. P. in *"apprendre, application"* etc. T.T in *"attraper, attaquer"* etc. and sometimes more rarely C.C. *"accroistre"*, D.D. *" addresser"*, G.G. *"aggreger"*, etc. And the following syllables: DE. *"de deffendre, de detacher"*, etc, LELE. *"le lendemain"*, MEME *"me mesprendre"*, SESE. *"se separer"* etc.

In the Spanish language, this doubling is not so frequent, but sometimes we find FF. *"offrecer"*, NONO. *"nonobstante"*, SESE. *"senalo"*, etc.

<u>Sixth observation</u>

To detect which of the proposed denotations will be the correct one, when we are confronted with a cipher, we must assume and compare one syllable after another before we will arrive at the one true meaning of the letter or syllable. Even if the same syllable is repeated twice within another ciphered syllable, the one that we see the most and has the most contacts with other syllables and has the same letter, we shall infallibly recognize their true meaning by the negation view which we explained in the preceding chapters, and that is also useful for the decryption of the composite ciphers.
That will never fail in helping one to find the truth that is sought and it may be said that this is the main secret in the art of deciphering. And he will know much more particularly by the examples which will be given later on, and we will also show the reason for this infallibility.

<u>Seventh observation</u>

When one sees the same number arranged in such a way that it precedes and immediately follows another, like this: 30. 15. 30. Then there is reason to believe that it is in French the syllable *"me"*, and the cipher character which is in the middle signifies S. *"mesme"* or *"que"* which is in the middle of *"quelque"* or *"te"* which has a S. in *"teste"* or X. in *"prétexte"* or *"che"* together with R. in *"chercher"* or *"re"* with P. in *"repre"* and so on.

And in Spanish ciphers we see a similar character as with *"de"* and S. in the middle in the word *"desde"* and *"la"* with P. in *"la placa, la planta"* and *"ta"* with N. in *"tanta"* and finally *"re"* with P. in *"reprenter, represalla"*. (33vo)

<u>Eighth observation</u>

When we notice a cipher character is repeated two or three times at a certain distance, which corresponds to the situation of the syllables which are also repeated in some words in Spanish or French, it is an almost inescapable mark that the cipher characters represent the same word, or at least one can make the assumption that a standard decryption operation starts there; for example if I noticed the following characters somewhere: 65. 24. 65. 18. 12. 65. where the number 65 is repeated three times at a distance which corresponds to the syllable *"re"* in the word of *"reprendre"*.

I have then reason to assume that 65 would mean *"re"*. 24-p. 18-n. 12-d. and according to this assumption I can make all my subsequent reasonings, and continue the course of this operation, and compare them with other characters in other places according to the preceding observation, until I see that I mistakenly assumed it, seeing any contradictions in the results.

<u>Ninth observation</u>

Sometimes a cipher character that is very seldomly used can prove to be useful during decryption.
It can give the conjecture of the meaning of some other characters, on where this character is attached, for example if it is near a character of which I suspect to know what it is, like a B. a G., or a X. These are rarely seen in a ciphered letter.

It gives me opportunity there to recognize others which are more significant, if it is a B. then it's necessary that the following syllable is one of the following five: *"la. le. li. lo. lu."* or one of these: *"
ra. re. ri. ro. ru. ou sa. se. si. so. su."* or finally *"ta. te. ti. to. tu."*. If it is a G. the characters that follow will be *"la. le. li. lo. lu . na. ne. ni. no. nu."* or *"ra. re. ri. ro. ru."*. If it is a X. then the following is *"
"pe. pi. pu. po. pre."* or *"pri. ta. ou te. tra. ou tre."* or *"ce"*. The character that which precedes it, must ordinarily be an E.
From which may be inferred that everything in a ciphered letter may help us in its own ciphering, since often the least used characters make us familiar with the most significant ones.
Sometimes a point that the encryptor has placed inattentively, shows use the end of a word or a line. A sharp accent that he placed on a character will signal to us, that it is a syllable, for example as in the last letter in these words: *"nécessité, trompé, réparé"*, etc.

This minor detail caused once that a letter from the Resident of France at Liège was easily deciphered, which on itself was very well encrypted. The discovery of an X. inside caused that another letter was deciphered from Marquis de Louvoy [58] written to Marshal Estrade [59] in such a way that a decipherer can't ignore. He must observe everything, up to the slightest accent and punctuation, being very sure that the slightest trivial thing can start very considerable conjectures. (34vo)

image: François Michel Le Tellier, Marquis de Louvois. (left) and Goderfroi d 'Estrades (right). source Wikipedia

Tenth observation

When we once know a plain character or we have reason to believe that it is what we think it is, we can decide it based on the predecessor or successor, by the other letter relations, or by certain syllables, or it has the best connection with the strength table, that it complies with all the conjectures and rules. For example, when we once know N., and that the cipher character which follows it

---

[58] Michel Le Tellier, Marquis of Louvois (1639-1691), Secretary of State of War, (Secrétaire d'État à la guerre) then Chancellor of France (1677). Minister of war, he raised and organized the armies of Louis XIV and can be considered as the creator of the military institutions of France. He was the resolute opponent of Colbert.

[59] Godefroid-Louis, Count of Estrades (1607-1686), Diplomate and Marshal of France, negotiated the Treaty of Nijmegen (1678). He was the friend of 'grand pensionary' Jean de Witt and the pensionaries of Amsterdam and of 's-Hertogenbosch. In Dutch this is "raadspensionaris Johann de Wit", at that time the name for a function what we would now know as prime minister. (DS)

in French has a big strength, we have reason to believe that it is S. Such as in *"actions, fortifications, sans, dans"*, etc. Or T. as in *"ment, tant, donnent, sont"*, etc. Or the syllable *"de"* as in *"grande, monde"*, etc.

If the strength is average, we could take *"ce"* as in *"prince, province, France"*, etc. or take *"ne"* as in *"donne, personne"* or *"te"* as used in *"santé, bonté"*, etc.

In all these cases the preceding character must be either a vowel or at least it's a syllable that ends in a vowel. And in order to come to positive and specific knowledge between the choices and all alternatives, which we just have described, we must take the negative path of which we have spoken so often before, and which is the most universal way to guide and manoeuvre the operations of decryption.

Eleventh observation

When we notice two cipher characters, arranged such that one of them is in on the first and third place and the other on the second and the fourth like this example: 76. 32. 76. 32. the first must ordinarily signify *"che"* or *"me"*, and the second R. or S. as in *"chercher, mesmes"*, etc.

Twelfth observation

To recognize the characters that represent an entire word, we must consider look at those that are completely out of the reach for the others and those that seem not to be nulls. Because it is certain that there are whole words if the total table of 3-letter syllables exceeds 100 characters, for the Spanish language it is very rare that a syllable of three letters exceeds that number, like *"dar, der, dir, gaz, gez"*, etc. But we can't draw this consequence from the table of syllables of France, because most of them there exceed the total number of 100 and even sometime 500 or more.

However, one can draw to the same conclusion another way, because there is no need to observe the cipher characters which are repeated the least in a letter and these must not be joined to other letters, nor must they be nulls. With which we notice that they can't be part of a possible word, and they must be themselves a whole word, especially if they are followed and preceded by characters which one decided are signalling to be articles like *"la. le. de."*, etc. I have said when they must not be a cipher null and how to recognize those in the explained section before. [60] (35vo)

---

[60] See the beginning of Chapter II (DS)

Thirteenth observation

From the previous observation, it follows that when we know a whole word, or at least if we have some reasons for recognizing some articles that must follow or precede it, like: *"la. ville de... la place... ie Prince de..."*, and the SS. that follow and are found there always represent their plural.

Fourteenth observation

If during previous observations one thinks that a certain character should represent a syllable or a letter and that it is not yet certain, it can be compared with other cases where it is found and meets other characters. By the proprieties or incompatibilities that one notices there, one can decide to accept or reject the meaning that one would like to attribute to it, as was previously written during the treatment of simple ciphers.

Fifteenth observation

The null characters can be recognized the same way in the composites, as they can be in the simple ciphers. If we notice two or three characters used very often in the first and last articles and very rarely in the rest of the fabric of the letter, it is sufficient proof to assume that they are nulls.

Sixteenth observation

It is practically impossible to consider the previous observations in an encrypted letter, especially if it is long, and there are often several places where we see these encounters. It is also morally impossible to ask someone to apply these rules well, if he never deciphered a letter himself.
Nevertheless, there are still some precepts to be given, which will make it extremely easy to apply all these observations, and which contain the most secret mysteries of the art of deciphering. We will see the details in the following chapter, after which we will come to the proofs of all that has been advanced about the composite ciphers.

Chapter VI: Specific principles that facilitate the art of decryption

As usually happens in the composite ciphers which are those used in most of the Secretariats of Estates of Europe[61], there are several characters that signify each letter which are used most often, such as A. N. R. S. F. U. One of the biggest secrets in achieving success during deciphering is knowing what the cipher characters are that signify the same plain character, because in the case that we observe one by one, the true strength will reveal it and by that method we can easily decide which letter it is.
It is certain that in the Spanish language the consonant S. is the most repeated one, if we know all the other cipher characters, and we did not yet assign it to another character, we can recognize it by the many repetitions that are present together, which then can't be anything else than the S. (37)

First principle

One must go through the entire ciphered letter and notice all the places where the same characters are frequently repeated and are near itself, in the same and similar arrangement, and one must make sure that any changes are not only in appearance (because of the multiplicity of cipher characters that signify the same plain character), but the letter or syllable signified must always be the same, and one must not take all these different ciphers characters mixed with others in the same disposition and think they are the same letter, but judge each single character to its strength, as if it has the power of all these characters together. The cleverness behind this operation, or proposition, will be properly explained by an example.

I suppose now that the word "*operaciones*" is seen five or six times in a big Spanish letter, as it appears very often and the cipher characters of the intended key are meant to represent letters and syllables, so that this word is composed of these, such that they are marked as:

---

[61] Des Secrétaireries d'Estat de l'Europe (DS)

o	. . . .	4-9
pe	. . . .	46
ra	. . . .	55
ci	. . . .	37
ne	. . . .	26
s	. . . .	2-6-8

Moreover, I suppose that in the first and second occasion of the ciphered letter where this word is found, the official version has been ciphered like this: 4. 46. 55. 37. 4. 26. 2.; on the third occasion the letters will be varied and ciphered as: 9. 46. 55. 37. 9. 26. 6.; and on the fourth occasion the word will be: 4. 46. 55. 37. 9. 26. 6. and on the fifth and sixth place of word: 9. 46. 55. 37. 4. 26. 8.

I look at these seven ciphered characters carefully and I count four of them that are always the same on all six occasions of the despatch. On three others we see that often the same characters in the middle and the variated characters are the 4. and the 9. and the 6. 8. or 2.
Following that I make the reasoning (37vo) that in these seven characters always on four places the same can be found and on three other places other diversified characters are seen. But the same situation seems to occur and therefore I have reason to believe, that these seven figures signify nothing else but the same word, and consequently 4. and 9. represent the same character and that is for 2. 6. and 8. the same.

After this I counted all the strengths of these three ciphered characters 2. 6. 8., I have made a separate counting entity for each of them, by which I recognize almost what letter it signifies; as if 2. was repeated twenty times in the letter, 6. fifteen times and 8. thirty times; putting all these strengths together I would form one which would be worth sixty-five as if the strength of each of these three figures was sixty, whence I would have to conclude that the three can't signify anything else than the consonant S. and by the same method O. could be recognized. Then I look for a word in Spanish that could be represented by seven positions, of which the last is a S. and the first and fifth an O. Finding nothing else than these two here: *"oposiciones, operaciones"*, by which it now has become easy to know the true word.

This rule is so important that by this method one can say that the decipherer simply takes all composite characters and by that he will know all the ciphered characters which signify the same character.

And by this application and this precept one has decrypted in the Netherlands, after a period of four months, a letter from a Swedish Minister, who was in Paris, and wrote a ciphered letter to the Count of Rybenach [62]. Having noticed that in this letter the word *"Meclenbourg"* was repeated very often and that in the same situation the ciphered characters which signified *"Meclebourg"* [63], only those that signify N. and R. were not changed, by which they recognized the true strength of the characters, and what the two characters really are, and this made the decryption of the whole letter possible.

To counter this problem, the cipherer must be careful (when a word appears that must be repeated several times in his letter) to completely diversify all the characters of which it is composed,
or to diversify none: giving the decipherer many different changes or leaving him in the same uncertainty always.
But since those people that make the ciphered letters are often very ignorant in their own field, or careless in practicing all the rules of their art, it is unhealthy that this rule is not found in the few places in a long ciphered letter which one intercepts, in the few words that could show the practise of this important rule. (38vo)

Second principle

There are two kinds of numbers used in the Secretaries: those who use cipher tables with one order, used by the lesser gifted in ciphering, and those that represent syllables and proper words like *"ba. be. bi. bo. bu"*, etc., 25. 26. 27. 28. 29. Most of the cipher tables are of this type. The others that are the best and most assured have no ordering or if there is some, it is not natural but only artificial like:

ba.	be.	bi.	bo.	bu
42.	53.	64.	75.	86.

When one can distinguish, before beginning the operation of deciphering, what type of numbers there are in the table, which are used to quantify the characters

---

[62] Rübenach. (DS)

[63] In the original the "n" in the middle was omitted. It could be a mistake, but on the other hand it seemed to be a usual spelling for French to leave out the "n". See for example the "Corps universel diplomatique du droit des gens, 1739, Jean Du Mont". (DS)

in the encrypted letter, if it has numbers in a following order, this preliminary knowledge could serve as great help and could facilitate the one that applies it. Because it is very constant and, in that case, the single natural order of the numbers guides him gradually to the discovery of their meaning after knowing that or just one of the supposed.

And if the only arrangement of the numbers is together with their value, it show how to find a word which corresponds to it, similar like there is a letter in this ciphered word 56. 19. 67. 69. 37. 88.

If the table of the numbers is sequentially, since 67. and 69. immediately follow each other in the example proposed, also follow each other in their natural order, leaving a single space for another number between the two.

They signify two syllables that follow each other also in the same order, such a way that if 67 means "ma. na. sa. ta. etc" then 69 will mean "mi. ni. si. ti. etc"; if the first signifies "mi. ni. si. ti. etc" the second will mean "mu. nu. su. tu." and like this we could run through all the syllables that these two numbers could signify. We will then try to find a word which corresponds to it in this disposition, as we would ... [64]

On the other hand when we do not notice this conformity of strengths in the numbers corresponding to sequence of the most syllables, it is a signal that the cipher table does not follow that and there is no reason to believe we have to follow the height of the numbers, we only need to look at their strengths and their arrangement in which they are, compared to the others that accompany them, according to the rules given before, as these will shine less light on the decryption of letters.

But this is already something we should know, if the cipher does not follow this and we can't have fun with it by looking at the height of the numbers. These remarks are <u>very important</u>, and it is by this method that the letter which was sent to the Netherlands, and which showed to be ciphered, and was during two years in possession of the Secretary of State, that by order of His Majesty became the subject of this treatise and to make an Art of it.

---

[64] Here the text in the original manuscript has become unreadable.

<u>Third principle</u>

One of the important means of success during the decipherment of a letter lies in making well use of the suppositions and conjectures, and it can be said that this is the true key of this Art, just as an Astronomer would know how to make a good system when all his assumptions have been good. (39vo)

The decipherer inevitably arrives at the decryption of the despatch that he seeks, if he establishes his conjectures based on good principles and exact observations. Indeed, it is a sort of a system that he composes, enclosed by a scheme of the alphabet and which is still unknown to him, and to be fair, he must harmonize himself with all the dispositions and combinations of the various characters that are in the encrypted letter, in whatever places they are.
Like a good astronomical system, it must perfectly be suited to all the phenomena and appearances which arise from the situation of the stars and their movements, such that there is no phenomenon or effect in nature which could not be explained by the methods of a proposed system. And it must be an infallible proof, otherwise the suppositions upon which he based it, would be worthless.

In the Art of decryption this is the same because when one must follow de flow of the operation in this Art so that the meaning of a single character does suit the disposition in all the places inside the letter.

This is an obvious proof that if the first suppositions have been made wrong and if that the system is false, and the person who ciphered the letter would have mistaken himself and taken a character for another, which can be recognized afterwards by verification and by confronting the character with all the places of the letter where it finds itself in the letter, cause then the meaning by it should remain the same in all places and the same is true for all the other characters that accompany it. If there was made an error by the cipherer, this is then visible though any of these.

To make a good assumption, it must have these two qualities: a) it must be as simple as possible on itself, and b) must be the most fruitful and the most extended solution of the method and application used.

We know that the method of modern philosophy is much more correct and more straightforward than that of the old one, since very few principles are known by people, such as the understanding of the body, their faces, and their motions. It

68

explains with the utmost accuracy and admirable clarity all the effects of nature, notwithstanding their almost infinite variety.

Instead of the multiple principles the ancients used, the many qualities they imagined, the many hidden virtues, and finally the essence of being and half wisdom they produced without
necessity, can barely clearly explain the tiny effect that nature has had during the almost two thousand years and has given to them, in order to show them as way of speech, the torture of making a true application. (40vo)
Until then, it's needed most of the time to assign to each effect a particular principle,
and who is most often unknown and satisfies himself with saying that it's the property or the nature of such in producing such an effect without explaining, which is this nature, this and that property and particular principle, which is attributed to it, instead of using a single application from the general principles of modern philosophy, which are very simple, and in very small numbers, makes sense for everything that happens in nature, and therefore is so intelligibly that there are few people that that do not realize that.

This reflection may serve to make known when the principles, which are supposed to be true in the art of decryption, are indeed true or not, cause with lesser assumptions, a decipherer can explain more combinations. From the composite characters in an encrypted letter, it is certain that these same assumptions must be maintained and must be better and more infallible, than when it would be when a larger amount has to be used in order to explain fewer combinations.

From which it may be inferred, it is better to attach oneself first to the search for the characters which have the most power than to those who have the least. for with those they would be obliged to make more suppositions to explain less things.

From which we can infer that it's better to first focus on the search for the characters that have the highest strength, than those who have the least because with those we are impelled to make more assumptions and explain fewer things.

To arrive at the essence of this third principle, it is necessary to understand that two kinds of assumptions can be made during decryption of a letter: one is assuming that certain cipher characters signify certain plain characters, what may be called an affirmative assumption and the other that such and such cipher characters can't express such and such plain characters, which is a negative assumption.

The first is the easiest, the shortest and the best is use, and works in two directions:
knowing the strength, a cipher character and assuming that it must be a certain plain character, and the other is knowing the arrangement with other characters and the distance between them, so that there is reason to believe that they form a word cause the letters and syllables correspond to the same arrangement. For example, if there were the following cipher characters in this situation 36. 15. 36. 56. 12. 65. 36. One would notice that the number 36. is repeated in three places: the first, the third and the seventh. Looking for a word containing this syllable and repeated three times in the same form, I find the word "*representare*" may well be appropriate here. (41vo)

Therefore, I suppose affirmatively that 36. means *"re"*, 15-p, 56-se, 12-n, 65-ta, and I confirm this assumption and principle of my operation, noting that the character contacts of a ciphered letter where the same ciphered character is repeated often and close to another must be called the
weakness of the letter and it's by this that we usually start the decryption.

The second kind of assumption is the negative one, when we assume for example, that a certain ciphered character can't be such or such plain character for the reasons deduced in the preceding chapters. And after having assumed and verified by induction that it can't be indeed, one concludes what it must necessarily be.

This negative assumption is usually used only in two occasions. The first is when one has no reason to use the other, that is to say when the encrypted letter does not show any weakness, that is, when the ciphered characters found do not repeat themselves often near each other, and if there is no ciphered character whose strength is much different than that of all others; and as It may be that the letter could have been ciphered without such, the decipherment is more difficult. But with patience and application we will get at the end of everything.

The other occasion where we use a kind of assumption, is when we decide by the proposed rules that certain ciphered characters can only be such or such plain characters, because in this alternative way if we know what they do not represent, we will know what they are. We arrive at this point very often, so that the way of the negative assumption is the last important one in the Art of decryption.

Now, to use this negative assumption in the first place, we must focus on a particular ciphered character which has a strength equal to that of several others, also leaving in uncertainty several other characters equally in strength and taking all these characters one after the other of which we assume that it is some plain character. Until we find between them one that is not inconvenient, on different places and on its letter contacts, and we can be sure it is not one of the others. (42vo)

If by any chance the first character we choose, for determination of the proposed cipher by the method of the negation, seems to be a plain letter or a syllable that does not cause us inconveniences, we can hold on to our first assumption and confirm that it's a good and let the negative assumption conduct us in our successful operation, as we will see in the examples for the composite ciphers.

There only remains one thing to see before we start on these examples. Cause to explain a particular word that one recognizes in a certain place of a letter, there has been assumed a certain cipher character signifies a specific character, and by traversing all other places of the same letter which we did not notice before, we must find that the character fits with that assumption.
Then it's an almost demonstrative proof that the supposition has been well executed. It is like as during the explanation of the effects in physics; to explain something, we assume a certain cause that fits and using that we notice that the same cause explains perfectly also other effects, of which we did not think before we assumed. This is then a convincing proof that can be given for a real cause.

When for example we want to explain a particular property to a layman, which is that of the attracting iron by a certain side, or that of a turning needlepoint towards a stick that is rubbed, we assume that it is caused by magnetic channelling from the poles of the earth and which enters the pores of the layman the same way that faith does, and this assumption could very well explain one or two specific effects for him. But it must be noticed that the same cause with the same clearness also explains other effects and other properties of which the layman did not think of at first. Like that of repulsion or attraction by a side made from iron, and because of this one would see these properties.

It is certain that the same cause also explains all similar effects, and which have not been imagined at first and by only to explaining a few must be regarded as the true cause, because it does not seem possible that luck alone can't make other usages possible, other than those to which it was destined, unless the truth itself produced this uniformity.

Hopefully you will forgive this side-track in which we have insensibly been engaged, because it bares relevance to the subject we are dealing with.   (43vo)

Chapter VII: Application of the previous rules concerning the composite cipher

Like those examples given for the decryption of the simple ciphers where we verified the axioms and the rules that were established for that kind of encipherment, it is necessary here to use the same for the composite ciphers, which are the most important cipher, the most difficult and almost the only ones used by the Secretaries.   And so that nothing is missing from all that what is believed to contribute to the completion and accuracy of this work, examples will be proposed for the French language, and the Spanish language, as well as for practical usage of the simple ciphers.

<u>First problem : Decipherment of a Spanish composite cipher</u>

```
13 . 16 . 3̶0̶ . 28 .  6 . 26 . 78 .  5 . 31 . 3̶8̶ .  5 . 30 .  1 . 75 .  6 . 26 . 43 .  3 . 97 . 2̶6̶ .
10 . 67 . 11 . 98 . 2̶0̶ . 27 .  5 . 69 .  3 . 98 . 43 .  6 . 26 . 45 .  q . 78 .  5 . 17 . 51 . 87 .
56 . 28 . 2̶1̶ . 12 . 46 . 96 .  6 . 51 . 50 .  6 . 50 .  5 . 67 .  3 . 69 .  6 .  o . 50 .  6 . 60 . 67 .
2̶5̶ . 91 . 98 . 78 . 75 .  4 .  8 . 37 . 45 . 67 . 58 . 44 .  6̶ . 26 . 66 . 76 .  1 . 45 .  3 . 75 .
 5 . 27 .  8̶ . 85 . 36 .  d . 51 . 88 . 9̶6̶ . 80 .  5 . 50 . 45 .  6 . 56 . 99 . 85 .  3 . 45 . 67 .
58 . 35 .  5 . 40 . 75 .  1 . 45 .  5 . 26 . 75 .  5 . 91 . 20 .  5 . 50 . 46 .  d .  4 . 46 . 71 . 47 .
 3 . 75 .  5 . 13 . 3̶0̶ . 16 .
```

Suppose we must decipher this text in Spanish. We must first decide whether it is a simple or a composite cipher. The variety of the characters pass the number of fifty, and now we know at the beginning it is a composite type. Then we examine the strengths of each ciphered character in the same way as we should do for a simple cipher and at the same time we check, as proposed in the second principle, whether we can detect in the table a kind of a sequence, which is done in the following manner.   (44vo)

No.		Count	No.		Count
1	+++	3	43	++	2
3	++++++	6	44	+	1
4	++	2	45	++++++	6
5	++++++++++++	12	46	+++	3
6	++++++++	8	47	+	1
8	+	1	50	+++++	5
10	+	1	51	+++	3
11	+	1	56	++	2
12	+	1	58	++	2
13	++	2	66	+	1
16	++	2	67	+++++	5
17	+	1	69	++	2
20	+	1	71	+	1
21	+++++	5	75	++++++	6
27	++	2	76	+	1
28	++	2	78	+++	3
31	+	1	80	+	1
35	+	1	85	+	1
36	+	1	87	+	1
37	+	1	88	+	1
40	+	1			

No.		Count	No.		Count
91	++	2	20	+	1
96	++	2	26	+	1
97	+	1	21	+	1
98	+++	3	30	++	2
99	+	1	d	++	2
6	+	1	o	+	1
8	+	1	q	+	1

In this table we notice in the first place, that only a few composite numbers that end with 4. and 9. and none ending in 2., but mostly in 0. , by 1., by 5., by 6., and by 8.

This agrees with what we discussed in the second principle; to recognize the table and a sequence within where many ciphered characters have an endings ion 2. 4. and 9., corresponds to plain text syllables ending in i. or U., which are the least frequent ones and the others with the plain text syllables ending in A. in E. and in O. which are seen quite often. So, I have reason to believe that there is a sequence in the table of the cipher, and thus I search for the key, which will shine a little light on the decryption. Then I recognize that the characters that have the most strength are the following: 5. repeated twelve times, 6. eight times[65], 3. six times, 45. six times, 75. six times, 26. five times, 50. five times.

5	+ + + + + + + + + + + + _	12	75	+ + + + + + _ _ _ _ _ _ _	6
6	+ + + + + + + + _ _ _ _ _	8	21	+ + + + + _ _ _ _ _ _ _ _	5
3	+ + + + + + _ _ _ _ _ _ _	6	50	+ + + + + _ _ _ _ _ _ _ _	5
45	+ + + + + + _ _ _ _ _ _ _	6	67	+ + + + + _ _ _ _ _ _ _ _	5

According to the second and third observation it is necessary that the consonant S. represents one of these seven characters, which have the most strength, and that five or six of the following letters or syllables will follow: "r. n. de. do. la. lo. no. que. re. ta. te.", etc. These will be assigned to the other ciphered characters, and are not assigned to S., which is valid for most of them.

Having proposed that, I now point my eyes to the whole cipher article and try to see if there is any weakness, where I could start my operation and use the affirmative assumption of which is spoken in the third principle. When I first notice that the three ciphered characters 13. 16. et ~~30.~~ are placed in the beginning and on the end of the text, without being repeated anywhere, it makes me wonder if they are nulls.

Now in the second place, I take notion that at the end of the third line there are these numbers: 50. 6. 50. 5. which gives me reason to believe, by the sixth observation, that the numeral 50. represents the syllable *"de."* and 6-S and there is the word *"desde"* or 50. means *"ra."* or *"re."* and 6-P. *"lapla.., repre…"* or finally that 50. means *"ta."* and 6-N *"tanta"*. As third remark I see that the two ciphered characters that follow up each other the often are 75. and 5. which are found in three places of the text in the same situation, which makes me decide by the fourth observation that these could mean: the first *"co."* and the second *"n."*. Or the first *"la."* or *"lo."* or *"ne."* and the second forms one of these syllables: *"la-s, lo-s, mo-s"* or *"ne-s"*. (45vo)

If the ciphered text will be understood better, it will undoubtedly show a lot of weak points where we can discover its key, but now we work with these two or three observations that we got, and we will now see how we can proceed with them.

---

[65] although in original image showed 6 and not 8. corrected. (DS)

If 50. means "*de.*" and 6. means S. and therefore the word "*desde*" represents these three characters 50. 6. 50. It's signalled by the number 5. , which is found directly after it and has the highest strength [66] in the entire ciphered text. According to its strength it should mean "S. R. N. de. do. la. lo. que. re." or it can no longer express S. since we assigned that to the 6. and the consonant S. cannot follow the word "*desde*" when the total cipher is composed through syllables. By the same reasoning we can say that it can't be N. nor R. because it can't be "*desder. desder*". It will not be able to represent the syllables "do. re. ", etc. because of the same inconvenience. There remains only these "la. lo.", which can mean the "*desde la… desde lo... desde que…*"

But as from the third remark, it has been conjectured that 5. who follows 75. several times must form together with that, one of the syllables "co-n, la-s, lo-s, mo-s, ne-s" and hence it must be N. or S. And it can't signify "la, lo, que", since the same S. is found at the end of the text on the place which immediately precedes the ciphered characters 13. ~~30.~~ 16. of which is suspected these are nulls.

We can therefore conclude by the negative view that because of all these inconveniences there can't be "*desde*" on the place where these 50. 6. 50. are. And that 50. does not mean the syllable "de.".
We must now see if it could mean "la." or "re.". But as in both cases of the ciphered character 6. that is between two, should signify P. "la pla ... repre…" and that furthermore there are high strengths on the letters N. R. and many syllables must precede it in strength. It is not likely that there are any more of these two half words as "la pla ... repre ... " in this manner, and now we are left with the word "*tanta*", which can be there based on the 6th observation.

And that seems to be the most probable in this case of 6. signifying N. to which his strength seems to be N. and 5. could be S. and in that case we would see there:

ta. n. ta. s.

50. 6. 50. 5.

(46vo)
If 5. means S. and if there is nothing more apparent and that the strength of the

---

ciphered character in the whole text and very often joined to 75. and can consequently form with it one of the syllables "la-s, lo-s, mo-s, ne-s", then there is nothing that rejects our supposition.

Coming to those that must be looked at the ciphered characters 75. 5. of which we can say that they must express one of these syllables "la-s, lo-s, mo-s, ne-s", where the first syllable is already excluded by the preceding reasoning, where it has been concluded that 5. should mean S. or N.
But now it's the difficulty of guessing right amongst the remaining four, because it seems that each of these four is equally suitable.

Though if we reflect on our observations above, that the table of the cipher and the order of the syllables could apparently have a sequence, we can conclude from it that 50. 6. 50. 5. signifies *tantas* , formed by this reasoning: if 50. signifies "ta." and that the syllable table has each time five and five syllables, it appears that we can apply our "first observation" as explained before; all the syllables that have an ending in A. can be expressed by a ciphered character whose second character will be zero as 50. 60. 70. etc., or 5. as 65. 75. 85. since it is the fifth ciphered character after zero.

The syllables ending in E. can be expressed by the numbers whose second number will be 1. or 6. like 51. 56, and the syllables with ending I., by 2. or 7., like 52. 57. etc., those ending in O. by 3. or 8., as in 53. 58. and finally those with U. by 4. or 9. as like 54. 59. etc.

Thus, having proposed, for the number 75., which precedes 5. so often of who we think it is an S. , could represent a syllable ending in A., and as we already recognized, it can only represent "*la, lo, mo, ne*" so it can make with S. these "*la-s, lo-s, mo-s, ne-s*". It follows from this that it will signify "la" because it is the only one of the four that has an ending in "a", and that therefore 76. will mean "le", 77-li, 78-lo and 79-lu as 51. will mean "te", 52-ti, 53-to, 54-tu, which must give big insights for successful completion of the proposed problem.
Provided that the first suppositions are true so that we can check it by placing each known character on the cipher and see if we get a sensible text or parts of useful text and not gibberish.

But to conduct this operation more successful, I have yet another conjecture, derived from the three ciphered characters that appear at the beginning of the ciphertext, immediately after the first three of which I think they are nulls. (47vo) These three figures are 28. 6. 26. and I think, since in previous conjectures the ciphered characters where the second one is a 6., must be a syllable that ends in E. And where the second character is a 8. must signify something that ends in O. and furthermore I already know that the 6. which is between 28. and 26. expresses the consonant N.

It is now necessary that I search for a word in all possible combinations of the alphabet whose first syllable ends in O. followed by a N. and then followed by a syllable ending in E. and corresponds with its consonant. The first must end in O. as the number 26. corresponds to 28. , so that if one is *"co."* the other must be *"ce."*, if one is *"mo."* the other must be *"me."*, etc.

And going through all the syllables in the alphabet I establish the following alternatives: these three digits 28. 6. 26. must mean one of the following words: *"bombe, conce, donde, fonfe, gonge, nomme, nonne , pumpe, ronre, sonse"*, because they can't mean *"lonle"* or *"tonte"* because we conjectured previously 78. meant *"lo"* and 76. *"le"* as 53. means *"to, 51. "te"* and among the half-words on which reported before, that we could make by going through the possible syllabes in the alphabet, there are not more than two that can be used to form a Spanish word: *"conce..."* and *"donde"*.

It remains to be seen which of the two is truly represented by these numbers 28. 6. 26.

For that we need to examine the figures that follow them, and these are 78. 5. because we already suspect what was said about the 78. expressing *"lo"* and 5. being S. and it follows that the five numbers 28. 6. 26. 78. 5. must form one of these words. *"donce los"* or *"donde los"*. But as the first isn't correct in the Spanish language, we know that *"donde los"* is the true meaning of those numbers and therefore 26. means *"de"* and 28. *"do."* From here I have reason to believe that 25. signifies *"da"*, 27. *"di"* and 29. *"du"*. and I believe now I know the following letters and syllables: N. S. da. de. di. do. du. la. le. li. lo. lu. ta. te. ti. to. tu.. By these methods we can now come to the knowledge of others, by putting them each on the ciphered character of which we suspect they represent it and see how they are found in the example of the problem in the following way as we will now show, in order to choose and see if any of our suppositions are true or false.

```
 _    _    _    do   n    de   lo   s              s                   ta   n    de
13 . 16 . ~~30~~ . 28 . 6 . 26 . 78 . 5 . 31 . ~~38~~ . 5 . 30 . 1 . 75 . 6 . 26 . 43 . 3 . 97 . ~~26~~ .

                di   s                        n    de             lo   s         te
10 . 67 . 11 . 98 . ~~20~~ . 27 . 5 . 69 . 3 . 98 . 43 . 6 . 26 . 45 . q . 78 . 5 . 17 . 51 . 87 .

      do                   n    te   ta   n    ta   s                   n         ta   n
56 . 28 . ~~21~~ . 12 . 46 . 96 . 6 . 51 . 50 . 6 . 50 . 5 . 67 . 3 . 69 . 6 . o . 50 . 6 . 60 . 67 .

            lo   la                            de                            la
~~25~~ . 91 . 98 . 78 . 75 . 4 . 8 . 37 . 45 . 67 . 58 . 44 . ~~6~~ . 26 . 66 . 76 . 1 . 45 . 3 . 75 .

 s   di                  te              s    ta        n
 5 . 27 . ~~8~~ . 85 . 36 . d . 51 . 88 . 96 . 80 . 5 . 50 . 45 . 6 . 56 . 99 . 85 . 3 . 45 . 67 .

       s         la            s    de   la   s              s    ta
58 . 35 . 5 . 40 . 75 . 1 . 45 . 5 . 26 . 75 . 5 . 91 . 20 . 5 . 50 . 46 . d . 4 . 46 . 71 .

       la   s    _    _    _
47 . 3 . 75 . 5 . 13 . ~~30~~ . 16 .
```

After having made this overview where I can't yet notice any contradiction, the syllables, and letters here are arranged such that they can be used to form whole words, and therefore I have reason to believe that I am not mistaken in my assumptions, and I continue the same path, by focussing on the places where I can easily make words and I notice there two in the first line:

```
lo        s                   s
78 . 5 . 31 . ~~38~~ . 5 .
```

and the second one on the 4th line:

```
ta   n    ta   s              n         ta   n
50 . 6 . 50 . 5 . 67 . 3 . 69 . 6 . o . 50 . 6 . 60 . 67 . ~~25~~ . 91 .
```

I think on it and in the first place if the ciphered characters whose second number is 1. represent syllables that end in E. and those whose second number is 8. represent those that end in O. analogue on that conjecture.
It is necessary that 31. means the *"le"* or *"ce"* or *"fe, ge, he, me, ne, pe, que, re, se, ve, che"*, and that 38 signifies *"bo, co, cho, fo, go"*, etc. and that there are more characters in disguise.

```
lo
78 . 5 . 31 . ~~38~~ . 5 .
```

One of the following words: *"los becos, los befos, los bechos, los begos, los bernas"*, etc. and the others that can be formed by this combination, assuming that for 31. = *"be"* there are no significant words here, I move on to the next assumption when 31. could mean: *"ce"* as in *"los cefos, los cegos, cemos, cenos, cepos*, etc. And perhaps 31. fits *"fe"*, for making: *"los febos, los fegos, femos"*, etc. and there are more possible but there I did not find significant words.

Going through the possible combinations I find that there is no better word for these than

lo   s   s

78   .   5 . 31 . ~~38~~ . 5 .

as in *"los hechos"* where I see that 30. 31. 32. 33. 34. could represent ha. he. hi. ho. hu. and 35. 36. 37. 38. 39., cha. che. chi. cho. chu. After this I move on to the second remarkable place where these ciphered characters are:

ta   n   ta   s   n   ta   n

50 .   6 . 50 .   5 . 67 .   3 . 69 .   6 .   o . 50 .   6 . 60 . 67 . ~~25~~ . 91 .

and I pursue my reasoning that way.

All the preceding operations convinced me that the table of the ciphered characters must follow this scheme above, and we see that the syllables ending in A. expressed by numbers end in zero or in 5. and the syllables ending in E. by cipher in 1. or in 6. and furthermore, derived from that the 67. which is in the beginning of the word and during a search we find a syllable that ends in "i", and the cipher 69. points at u., the number ~~25~~. is a syllable ending in a. and the number 91. an ending in E.   (49vo)

Because of the word *"tantas"* in the beginning I start to look for the termination of the word, and where there must be an "as." or "es.". Like *"ta-ntas, cosas, tantas operaciones"*, etc. and finally I see the word that I am looking for, which must have its first syllable ending in u. and which corresponds to the first like 69., corresponds to 67. that this syllable is followed by N. as single letter. Pursuing this method, I notice the syllable "ta." and the consonant N. close to each other and which are already known, and they end there in syllable with i.

80

and it's the same character 67. and in the end this syllable follows another which has the vowel A. and corresponds to the end of the word *"tantas"* which it precedes, it looks like the last syllable of the word that we look for is "as." and that this must be expressed by a single ciphered character; since I do not notice in any reason in this place any character which must signify S.

After all these conditions being established, I search in all the Spanish words which come to mind, for a form or a word that holds all that I have just reported on and after having traversed between all the combinations of the syllables I did not find a more suitable one than the word "circunstancias".
So that I have reason to believe that 67. means "ci." and 69., or ~~25,~~ is "as", and that the letter o. is a second ciphered character that represents, yet again S., and finally 3. signifies r. and I have more reasons to believe now that this ciphered character [67] is one of the letters that has the third strength, and that the letters N. and S. are already known.

On this strong supposition with high reliability, I make the a new overview: [68]

```
        _    _    _   do   n   de   lo    s   he  cho    s   ha        la    n   de          r          es
13  .  16 . ~~30~~ . 28 .  6 . 26 . 78 .  5 . 31 . ~~38~~ . 5 . 30 . 1 . 75 .  6 . 26 . 43 .  3 . 97 . ~~26~~ .

                      di    s   cu    r              n   de             lo    s         te
10  .  67 . 11 . 98 . ~~20~~ . 27 . 5 . 69 .  3 . 98 . 43 . 6 . 26 . 45 . q . 78 .  5 . 17 . 51 . 87 .

        do                   n   te   ta    n   ta    s   ci    r   cu    n    s   ta    n   ci
56  .  28 . ~~21~~ . 12 . 46 . 96 .  6 . 51 . 50 .  6 . 50 . 5 . 67 .  3 . 69 . 6 . o . 50 .  6 . 67 .

as            lo   la                ci              de   ce   le              r   la
~~25~~ . 91 . 98 . 78 . 75 . 4 . 8 . 37 . 45 . 67 . 58 . 44 . ~~6~~ . 26 . 66 . 76 . 1 . 45 . 3 . 75 .

 s    di                 te                s   ta    n                r        ci
 5  . 27 . ~~8~~ . 85 . 36 . d . 51 . 88 . 96 . 80 . 5 . 50 . 45 . 6 . 56 . 99 . 85 . 3 . 45 . 67 .

        s         la              s   de   la    s              s   ta
58  . 35 . 5 . 40 . 75 . 1 . 45 . 5 . 26 . 75 . 5 . 91 . 20 . 5 . 50 . 46 . d . 4 . 46 . 71 .

        r    la    s    _    _    _
47  .  3 . 75 . 5 . 13 . ~~30~~ . 16 .
```

---

[67] during translation it has not become clear to me which 'this' refers to (DS)
[68] the number 60. was removed in the sequence ta-n-ci. 50.6.67 (DS)

Like this it is very easy to find the letters and syllables that are unsolved. For example, where we see:

di   s

27 . 5 . 69 . 3 . 98 .

and we can decide that 98. means "so." for making this word *"discurso"* and by that, we come to know that 95. 96. 97. 98. 99. mean "sa. se. si. so. su.". The place where we have:

de   ce   le   r   la   s

26   . 66 . 76 . 1 . 45 . 3 . 75 . 5 .

we can decide that 1. means C. and 45.-ra., to form these words of *"celebrarlas"* by which we understand that 45. 46. 47. 48. 49. represent "ra. re. ri. ro. ru." such a way that there is nothing more difficult in the remainder of this ciphered piece and we can now present the total cipher the following way:

"Donde los hechos hablan de porsi es ocioso al discurso ponderarlos y teniendo el presente tantas circunstancias que solo la admiracion puede celebrarlos dignamente no se gastaran en su narracion mas palabras de las que bastaren a referirlas".

Which are the words of the first article of the relation that is printed a while later on the success of the 14[th of] August [69]. These words have been used to show that the examples given in the problems of this treatise, are not imaginary ones and can be used to apply the rules and propositions on the spirit of the language and can be used to decipher any kind of text.

---

[69] A search did not reveal to which exact document this is referring. It seems probably to me that it concerns the Franco-Dutch war, see later in the comments. The final Treaties of Peace of Nijmegen were series of documents, of which the first was signed on 10th August 1678. The last major battle in this war was fought on 14th August 1678 between the Dutch/Spanish and the French, in the Belgian place Saint-Denis, where some parties were unaware of the treaty and others ignored it. See Wikipedia. More research possible on f.e. de Yale law & diplomatic documents online here. (DS)

<u>Notes on the previous problem</u>

First, we observe that the previous example is too short, to give a good method on the decryption of a composite cipher, and that it was not a strong encrypted and once we there noticed the word "*tantas*" we solved the conjecture pretty quickly. It would have been much more difficult if the key to solve is longer, but if the text is longer, we find more repetitions of these characters and it would be easier to apply all the rules and observations that has been given.

Secondly, we recognize in our example that the weakest conjecture must yield to the strongest in terms of decryption, since the strongest presumption outweighs the weakest in terms of law, since by the third observation the number 50. , being the 6th or 7th in strength, must signify apparently one of the following syllables: "de, do, la, lo, no, que, re", etc.

But as by the 6th observation and the reasoning that we formed therein, it appears that the same number 50. should mean "ta" and none of the syllables mentioned in the 3rd observation and moreover of this conjecture has been supported by the number 6. and the number 5.
Their significations in the supposition of the word "*tantas*" appeared to be very probable, and the conjecture drawn from the 6th observation, to prove that the figure 50. represents "ta." was prevalent over that of the 3rd observation which gave rise to the assumption that this character should represent one of the syllables "de. do. la. lo. no. que. re. , etc.

Joint only when there are two different suppositions to be applied to the same character; where one is vaguer than the other and contains more alternatives. It is necessary that one is less important than the other, and it is necessary that the one with fewer limitations prevails, and the lesser undefined and uncertain one always contains less appearance of truth, which is the same certainty as in principle of metaphysics, where the three transcendental properties of the being "unitas, veritas, bonitas" [70], are always together, and it follows from it that the truth is inseparable from unity, and is consequently contrary to multiplicity, which is the only cause of uncertainty.

---

[70] These terms from the Franciscan saint Bonaventure (1221-1274), we consider these now both biblical as well as philosophical categories (DS)

On the third place the conjecture that we made based on the cipher table follows from the order of the syllables and the joined syllables, has contributed much to the discovery and to the perfection of the methods. Still, it is necessary to show another example of a Spanish cipher, which does not have an apparent weakness.

But as this example would become very long and besides that, the current treatise is already very long, we considered it more appropriate to abandon that idea, especially as the French cipher that we now will show, may be able to compensate a part of what is missing here.   (51vo)

I say that in the example that we will propose, there is not an apparent weakness, and because it is certain that for the decryption of a letter that does not have much weakness, and when the table with the strengths is without order and provides no success, we need to look at the circumstantiality of it, so that we can detect the key to decryption.
By deciphering the example of this problem, it is easy to mould the key, which was used in this cipher.

Second problem

A French cipher composed in June 1676, will be decrypted. The letter was intercepted in the Netherlands and taken from a French courier who was delivering the letter from the Christian King [71] to his ambassadors in Nijmegen[72]. The original that is in the hands of the author of the present work. [73]

---

[71] This must be the Sun King, le Roi Soleil, Louis XIV of France. One of his official titles during 1643-1715 was 'His Most Christian Majesty the King of France' (DS)
[72] This city played an important diplomatic role during this war, and it resulted in the Treaties of Peace of Nijmegen, a series of treaties signed in the period 1678-1679. The first negotiations for this began in 1676 and the ciphered document must have played a role of significance there. wikipedia (DS)
[73] From this note we can deduct that the writer was working for the Secretaries, which was very probable the Spanish one, which during those years supported the Dutch in their war against the French. See Wikipedia. (DS)

Image: The Coat of Arms of France. On the banner, the blue ribbon on the crown on top, we see the motto: "MONTJOIE SAINT DENIS". Representing the battle cry and motto of the Kingdom of France. The kings of France of that period were buried there. Source: Wikipedia, Grand Coat of Arms of France, and Navarre: from 1589 to 1790.

And as the cipher table, which these Ministries used for the safety of their despatches, was very elaborate and it seemed very difficult to decipher it, and an entire text will be given here, which will show where the subject of this problem lies.

This ciphertext is as follows:

```
1 67 2 44 16 44 69 14 89 2 12 94 40 18 38 44 16 46 69 38 34 61 39 53 6 43 6 14 98 20 43 10 89 18 10 75 16 14

71 31 62 31 15 99 95 6 13 19 49 20 49 12 19 11 19 12 50 10 20 98 19 2 18 46 24 46 39 1 69 53 10 32 2 38 71

12 19 1 75 12 75 38 89 18 71 97 73 26 46 19 96 31 38 98 ## 73 89 2 78 14 18 20 8 83 69 38 32 8 16 17 19 14 73

38 8 66 98 68 24 67 62 39 10 83 38 39 4 24 11 24 94 38 26 42 38 ## 38 32 34 67 16 46 89 98 68 44 16 44 69 14

## 2 25 36 94 38 89 34 61 2 18 20 16 76 44 39 79 59 81 20 46 64 2 25 2 12 21 6 6 97 6 26 89 14 5 6 5 96 62

38 9 19 24 13 83 98 36 14 98 73 20 89 75 2 21 89 22 14 71 6 13 19 59 15 24 53 46 6 14 16 2 4 76 18 95 14 20

73 20 89 81 1 2 85 16 35 1 61 2 18 20 6 21 6 40 98 4 47 10 44 24 26 ## 38 32 41 61 38 20 44 38 8 ## 64 98

29 38 2 13 21 6 44 19 25 38 69 14 20 69 44 14 24 44 10 75
```

To decipher this text, it is necessary to start with the same thing that has been practised in all the preceding problems, that is in order to recognize the strengths of each character and the relation of them towards the others, which is done the following way:

,,2	+++++++++++	11	..2	+	1
,,4	++	2	..9	+	1
,,6	+++++++	7	..6	+++	3
,,10	+++++++	7	..11	+	1
,,12	+++++	5	..12	+	1
,,13	+++++	5	..14	+	1
,,14	+++++++++++	11	..15	++	2
,,16	++++	4	..22	+	1
,,18	+++++	5	..24	+++++	5
,,20	++++++++++++	12	..26	+	1
,,24	I I I	3	..34	+++	3

etc.

On the following page I take the liberty to display the real, recalculated and sorted character frequency counts, and choose not use the original faulty one, which is partly displayed above. (DS)

cipher	repeated	cipher	repeated	cipher	repeated	cipher	repeated	cipher	repeated
,,38	18	71	4	_89	2	,,44	1	^25	1
,,20	12	,75	3	_96	2	,,64	1	^4	1
,,14	11	32	3	~1	2	100	1	_11	1
,,2	11	,,24	3	~16	2	11	1	_25	1
44	10	,,62	3	~5	2	12	1	_29	1
,98	9	_1	3	~94	2	14	1	_31	1
,,6	9	_26	3	15	2	2	1	_39	1
_19	8	_67	3	6	2	22	1	_41	1
89	8	34	3	97	2	26	1	_43	1
,,10	7	53	3	,42	1	35	1	_49	1
69	7	,76	2	,64	1	43	1	_73	1
,,18	6	,81	2	,68	1	47	1	_75	1
,,12	5	378	2	,78	1	49	1	_99	1
24	5	,,4	2	,79	1	50	1	~25	1
,39	4	,,40	2	,83	1	75	1	~31	1
,73	4	^18	2	,95	1	85	1	~46	1
,,13	4	^2	2	17	1	9	1	~6	1
,,16	4	_16	2	19	1	94	1	~66	1
_21	4	_36	2	31	1	95	1	~68	1
_61	4	_46	2	124	1	^14	1		
~8	4	_59	2	193	1	^16	1		
46	4	_83	2	,,32	1	^19	1		

After this table has been created, the first thing I notice is that the total amount of characters is very large; there is a great diversity of characters. The second remark is that apparently the characters that have two accents like `` above seem to mean single letters of the alphabet, because I notice that the column, where these kinds of characters are seen, is the one which contains most of the characters, which have the most strength. Also, these are one of those that have only a mediocre extent in the diversity of characters, they are constant in these two qualities and in the column of the alphabet these syllables distinguish themselves by being less frequent, but appear in large numbers.

cipher	repeated
„38	18
„20	12
„14	11
„2	11
44	10
,98	9
„6	9
_19	8
89	8
„10	7
69	7
„18	6
„12	5

The third deliberation that can be made is that the cipher table should not be followed closely since it seems almost all the numbers are use indifferently.

After these reflections it is necessary to review the characters which have the most strength, and they are the following ones, as displayed here in the short table. (53vo)

The way that by the 3rd observation of composite ciphers in the French language, the thirteen ciphered characters as in the above strength table, must represent the following characters and syllables, or at least a good part of "A. N. S. F. R. O. U. de. le. me. que. re. se. te.", etc, and there's reason to believe that the four first characters

„   „   „   „

38 20 2 14

must signify four of these five A. N. S. F. R.
since by the second remark they are in the column which appears to represent the single letters of the alphabet, and not those which express the syllables.

And if we want to step down to a more specific conjecture, we can be sure that

„

38

which is the character with the highest strength, must mean A. or S. or N., which are usually the letters that are most often repeated in the French language. If these conjectures are truth or false will be known through the following operations.

After these general reflections and alternative and indeterminate suppositions I investigate details of the ciphertext and try to recognize the weakest places, and which could provide the best grip, or starting point for my operation, and I notice in the first line the following characters

$$\begin{array}{cccccccc} ,, & .. & ,, & .. & .. & .. & .. & ,, \\ 2 & 44 & 16 & 44 & 69 & 14 & 89 & 2 \end{array}$$

that are in such an arrangement that they do not only give rise to the sixth observation, but also, like all the dangerous words that we reported here, there is nothing better suited for these eight numbers, than the words *"a présente a"*, according to the second remark which just has been made, the numbers

$$\begin{array}{ccc} ,, & ,, & ,, \\ 2 & 16 & 14 \end{array}$$

must represent single letters in the alphabet.
And the numbers

$$\begin{array}{ccc} .. & .. & .. \\ 44 & 69 & 89 \end{array}$$

must represent syllables, which follow the 3rd observation the best and must be syllables that have an ending in E., like "re. se. te.", etc., such that by this conjecture

$$\begin{array}{c} ,, \\ 2 \end{array}$$

represents A. And then

$$\begin{array}{ccccc} .. & ,, & .. & & .. \\ 44 = re., & 16 = p., & 69 = se., & 14 = ne.\ an & 89 = te \end{array}$$

When

$$\begin{array}{c} ,, \\ 2 \end{array} = A$$

then there is a great deal of likeness here, since not only does this fit very well in the text that we have, also that the same 2. has a strength that it must signify A. or N. or S. or F. or R. and none of these four last suits it very well. So the vowel A.

which is represents it, besides this number 2. is the first in the column, which is supposed to represent the alphabet of single letters, and that is our third convenience, which confirms the hypothesis that we established, that this number represents the first letter of the alphabet.

Then

$$\overset{..}{44}$$

signifies "re." because besides the conjecture we just formed. And there's another proof on another place in the ciphered text where we see a weakness, it's almost at the end of the last line where we see the numbers

$$\overset{..}{44} \quad \overset{,,}{14} \quad \overset{,,}{24} \quad \overset{..}{44}$$

that confirm the suspicion that the

$$\overset{..}{44}$$

signifies "re." because these four very strongly point at the words *"rendre"* or *"rentre"* without destroying any of the suppositions already made and confirm the previous rules; this explanation verifies and confirms the assumption we made in our second reflection, that all the numbers modified by these two accents ,, signify the single letters of the alphabet.
It also confirms that

$$\overset{,,}{14} = N$$

which also still is in line with the strengths of this cipher.
And now it's finally certain that all syllables that can represent

$$\overset{,,}{14}$$

which is according to the 6th observation *"me, te, che, re"*. There is none that will be suitable in this sequence

$$\overset{..}{44} \quad \overset{,,}{14} \quad \overset{,,}{24} \quad \overset{..}{44}$$

Because the

$$\overset{..}{44}$$

is already *"re."*. Which would mean that *"me, que, te, che"* according to the 6th observation, that there is only one character between these two that can make these words as *"mesmes, quelque, teste, cherche"*. But assuming that 44. means *"re."* there can very well be two characters between these two repetitions in the sequence that we have, such as in these words *"rendre, prendre, rentre"*, etc, where

$$'' = N$$
$$14$$

In addition to all the realities of the dispositions in which these numbers are found, it is clear from the strength table, that since we suppose that

$$'' = A$$
$$2$$

we can easily assume that

$$'' = N$$
$$14$$

It is found in the rank and strength necessary for that letter, and without other proofs that we have just given. So I suppose that by all these plausibility's the first line will represent the words *"a représente a"*. And then we see that the last line means *"rentre"* or *"rendre"*

$$.. \quad '' \quad '' \quad ..$$
$$44 \quad 14 \quad 24 \quad 44$$

Here are already two numbers which have a very high strength, for the A. and N.:

$$'' \quad \text{and} \quad ''$$
$$2 \qquad\qquad 14$$

And the three mediocre ones

$$.. \quad .. \quad ..$$
$$44 \quad 69 \quad 89$$

"rc. , se., te. ", and the lesser ones 16 - p. and finally another one that we think is T. or D:

$$''$$
$$24$$

But there are still two main ones that are

$$\underset{38}{,,} \quad \text{and} \quad \underset{20}{,,}$$

which according to their strength can be only S. F. or R. according to the third observation, since by the preceding conjectures A. and N. have already been excluded from their meaning. To discover the true meaning of these numbers, it is only necessary to look at the places where they are located near others who are already known and confront them with them. According to what is said in the 14th observation to determine what they are, because they can't be in accordance with the axioms of the negative proof that we have spoken of so often.

The place that can best help us find the meaning of these two characters is the last line, where they are located and look at them between those that we already know:

	se	n		se	re	n	d	re		
,,	..	,,	,,	..	..	,,	,,	..	,,	,
38	69	14	20	69	44	14	24	44	10	75

The disposition of these numbers may give reason to believe that

$$\underset{38}{,,} \quad \text{and} \quad \underset{20}{,,}$$

must be R. S. or F. And following our previous reasoning that R. and F. are not valid for 38. and S. and R. not for 20., then we can decide that

$$\underset{38}{,,} = S \qquad \underset{20}{,,} = F$$

Now it is certain that this 38. can't be R. nor F. anymore and this 20. can't be R. nor S. by the combination where these numbers are found on

	se		n
,,	..	,,	,,
38	69	14	20

In both cases there must be one of the four words that follow *"rsent, tsenr, rseris, ssenr"*, or they mean nothing; but here we know that 38. = S. and 20. = T. and that 24. = either T. or D. and nothing else but these, so the meaning of the other remaining ones already assigned to 20. and 38. will serve as proof for us. After the numbers 378 we see two occurrences of 38. (which one thinks to signify S.) and these give reason to believe that it must appear apparently in the plural form.

After all this having supposed, we now can give the following:

s	se	n	t	se	re	n	d	re		
,,	..	,,	,,	..	..	,,	,,	..	,,	,
38	69	14	20	69	44	14	24	44	10	75

This gives us enough on the cipher to make those words, and these suggest that we can make words as "*pussent, dussent*" or "*voulussent, se rendre*", etc. But we need more positions for the last one and the text does not provide us more letters after the 10.75. What could follow *“se rendre”* can be two words because those are the last ones there. The expression *“se rendre là, se rendre icy”* and also that

$$\begin{matrix} ,, \\ 10 \end{matrix}$$

is ”i.” or “l.” and that

$$\begin{matrix} , \\ 75 \end{matrix}$$

 is “a.”or “ci” or that the 10. is “la” and 75. is a null, are possibilities that we see here.

Let us now assume that

$$\begin{matrix} ,, \\ 2 \end{matrix} = A$$

as said before, and

N.	P.	S.	T.	RE.	SE.	TE.	i. L. or La	A. or Null
,,	,,	,,	,,	..	..	..	,,	,
14	16	38	20	44	69	89	10	75

And to clear any of our doubts we might have on these numbers, 10. and 75. we confront them with the other places in which they can be found. In the third line we find:

```
      t              te
     „     ··    „     ··    „     „     ,
    20    43    10    89    18    10    75
```

We think since 44. means "re", and since the 43. is before that number, it is plausible to believe that it must signify "ra", and by consequence then the meaning of 10. which is still unsure, must be fixed to a vowel i. , where the numbers

```
      t                te
     „     ··    „     ··    „
    20    43    10    89    18
```

of which there are already three known, can mean this word *"traiter"* like this:

```
    t    ra    i    te    r
   „     ··    „     ··    „
   20    43    10    89    18
```

and these two digits

```
    „     ,
   10    75
```

will mean this word *"icy traiter icy"* by which we come finally to the conjecture that 18., which was unknown, shows that we will gradually come to advance to parts of the cipher which have a high strength.

Having established all these conjectures, I aim at discovering yet more characters, and I search in the text that lies before me, for other places where some weakness by the mixture of numbers can reveal things to me, that are already known or related to them. There is one on the twelfth and thirteenth line where we find the following:

```
           r          n    t         t    te
   „    „    ,    ··    ,    ··    „    ,    „    ··
   2    4   76   18   95   14   20   73   20   89
```

on which I think that since 75. = ci., we could take the syllable "co" for the number 76. which immediately leads to think that we can bind the vowel "a." to the syllable "co", and it does necessarily need to be like this cause then 4. who is between the 2., which now is "a", and on the other side 76., of which we think could be "co", must now represent the consonant "c".

Then we have the half-word

a	c	co	r
ʽʽ	ʽʽ	ʼ	··
2	4	76	18

of which we already knew the 18.=R., and the consonants 14. 20. (who follow it at a close interval, with only the number 95. in between). It can be that the syllable "*da*" or "*de*" here is used for the words "*accordant*" or "*accordent*". And it follows that 95. will mean "da" or "de" and the three numbers

ʼ	ʽʽ	··
73	20	89

which immediately follow this word and of which the last two are already known to us, can only mean "*cette accordent, cette*", etc. It is now clear that there is no other syllable that is more suitable for forming something, and not we already have a half-proof to convince ourselves that 73. means "ce" since we recognized that 75. which is not very far away, means "ci".

All these conjectures are drawn from the 10th observation which speaks about the connection of letters and syllables. I still pursue to another remarkable place where the following characters are:

ʽʽ	··	··	··	··	_		ʽʽ		_	_	ʽʽ	ʽʽ	··	ʽʽ		~
4	47	10	44	24	26	378	38	32	41	61	38	20	44	38	8	193

and I say since 4. means C., 10-i. and 44-re., it is certain that 47. signifies "ro", to form this word:

c	ro	i	re
ʽʽ	··	ʽʽ	··
4	47	10	44

And there can be no other syllable assumed by the combination of the three, that are already known, other than 44=re, 47. that follows it closely may very well be the syllable "*ro*", of which we know that in the cipher table, the numbers do not always follow each other immediately when they signify syllables which follow each other. Which we already saw at 73. which is "ce" and 75 which is "ci", despite of the natural order which assumed this was 74.   (57vo)

But to return to the explanation of these numbers

```
  c   ro   i   re                s                s   t   re   s
  "    ..   ..   ..   ..   _         "        _   _    "    "    ..    "        ~
  4   47  10  44  24  26  378  38  32  41  61  38  20  44  38  8  193
```

Of course, it is evident that the number 24. following the word *"croire"* must mean *"que"* because we are having no other syllable available there which suits better there the connection of the text expected, and that there is a proper word on 378. that follows it almost immediately, which by the 13th observation makes us decide that the number 26., which precedes it, signifies an article *"le"* or *"les"* and there's enough reason to believe that it is indeed. Now we know that this proper word is in the plural form by the number 38., that means S. and that immediately follows 378.
There it seems to stand for the clean word *"prince"* or *"envoyé"* or *"ambassadeur"*, and in this letter where in the following line they speak of taking Nijmegen[74] it is likely that it represents *"ambassadeur"*.

I will therefore continue to make my conjectures the same way for this entire line and we see that between the word *"ambassadeur"* and the next half-word there are only these three numbers 32. 41. 61. Then I suspect that to make the connection between them, that the first is *"et"* and the second *"mi"* and the third *"ni"*, to make the word *"ministres"*, which gives all the more reason to be convinced by the previous observations that it is certain that 41. and 61. are syllables.
Between those that remain unknown there are not better suitable ones than these for the words *"ambassadeurs"* and *"ministres"*. These provide insight on the 8., which follows them, that it signifies one of them or alike because it precedes 193. There is reason to believe that it means another whole word, because it is outside the scope of the remaining numbers. Notice that in the last line the following numbers appear:

---

[74] in French: Nimmègue (DS)

s	se	n	t	se	re	n	d	re	i	ci
,,	^	_	,,	..	,,	,,	..	..	,,	,,	..	,,	,
44	19	25	38	69	14	20	69	44	14	24	44	10	75

and they must express these words *"pussent"* or *"dussent"* or *"voulussent se rendre icy"*, such a way that we only need to know the two or three first ones.

As it has been recognized above that

$$\overline{26}$$

means *"les"*, there is reason to believe that

$$\overline{25}$$

which precedes the half-known words above, it will mean *"lu, du"* or *"pu"* and consequently the word *"voulussent"* here fits best between the two others. Which let us suspect that

$$\overset{,,}{44}$$

signifies *"vo"* and 19-v. or 44. signifies U. or 19. is *"vou"* and 44. is as last option the ending letter of the previous word.

vou	lu	s	se	n	t
,,	^	_	,,	..	,,	,,
(44 19)	25	38	69	14	20

(58vo)
There is still some reasoning to be done, before moving on to other places in the cipher, since 26. seems to mean *"les"* and 25. *"lu"*, but 19. precedes them and has almost the same strength and could express easily one of these syllables *"de, le, me, que, re, se, te"*, etc.
This expresses the syllable *"le"* more probable than any of the others, since especially most of them are already known. By all the reasoning that we just made, it follows that we almost know the following letters and syllables: A. C. d. n. p. r. s. t. ca. ce. ci. co. cu. la. le. li. lo. lu. les. ma. me. mu. mo. mu. and because of *"mi."* we also have: na. ne. ni. no. nu. and because of "ni." we also have: ra. re. ri. ro. ru., sa. se. so. su. and because of "se.": ta. te. ti. to. tu. and because of "te. and "et" as reserve of it, also the conjunction "que". And between all the other ciphered characters we also need to know what is

To this we can arrive rather easily, as well as for all the other unknown numbers, if we make a plan of the whole cipher and mark on each character the related letters and known syllables.

And those for which we have reference to it or we can see based on their strength what they are, or by the sequence in the letters or word we can now make a new scheme of the cipher. (59vo)

In all these half-sentences and half-words it is very easy to make remaining letters and form whole words, by conjectures, assumptions and reasonings similar to those we did before. As for example that we know

,
95

means *"da."* and

—
19

means *"le."* It could furthermore be assumed that

, and —
98   21

who immediately follow these in the filled table, represent one of the next syllables very nearby, such as *"de."* or *"li.".* This way it is no longer difficult to discover the remaining characters, and it's certain that by these kinds of operations we need to have one good first discovery, and then by using the rules and by little application of the proposed logic, one will find the meaning of the whole ciphertext.

"Il nous est représenté [75] à plusieurs reprises qu'il n'y auroit pas moyen de traitter icy, si l'on estoit perpétuellement troublé par le bruit des armes, que mesmes il seroit impossible de subsister si tout ce qui fait le puys de Nimègue n'estoit à couvert des courses et des violences des gens de guerre que nous y avions autant d'intérest que tous les autres ambassadeurs et qu'il nous prioit de le représenter à Votre Ma.té qu'il s'y avoit encore aucun contribution establie

---

[75] This is the original text in the book, however there are some major incorrect issues here, which translated to another intention than the correct text. Which is presented and discussed by me in the appendix. (DS)

*dans toute l'estendue du pays pour lequel on demande cette neutralité et
qu'ainsy elle n'y perdrait rien en accordant cette condition sans la- quelle il n'y
avoit pas lieu de croire que les ambassadeurs et Ministres des Princes et de leurs
Alliés voulussent se rendre icy."* [76]

It is the translation from the decryption of the Ambassadors of France letter,
which has been chosen to serve as subject for this problem by which we will
finish the treatise on the method for the interception of composite ciphers from
the Secretaries, after that we will now make some reflections on the operations
we've just made.

For the final and correct decrypted letter, see the appendix. [77]

<u>Reflections on the previous problem</u>

One can see in the employment of this problem how one comes to the
knowledge of whole words or half-words which are being expressed by a single
character.

For the continuation of the treatise and as follow-up on the cipher where a
weakness has led to the exposure of the whole, after we discovered that

$$\frac{\_}{61} = ni \quad \text{and that} \quad \frac{\_}{67} = nous$$

and if the sense of communication of this treatise allows it, cause as it happens
in the beginning of the ciphered text, we have the words *"nous a représenté"* [78] ,
and by the same method we recognize

$$\frac{\_}{1} = il$$

and then by joined characters we get

---

[76] The text itself speaks of the fact that there is still no agreement in the 'country of
Nijmegen'. (DS)
[77] For the full transcript, decipherment, frequency and tables with n-grams and such,
please see the appendix. (DS)
[78] presented (to) us (DS)

which is *"intérest"*. Like this we recognize that

.. signifies *"pas"* and   .. = "pour"

6   9

By such linking we know now that [79]

..	= par,	..	= plus,	..	= paix,	..	= per,
11		12		14		15	

~	= gens,	~	= guerre,	~	= ge.
66		68		59	

And then there are the half-hearted words such as, *"oit, roit, tant, ment, ron, ter, vou"* and others that we notice during working on the problem.

---

[79] paix: At first this was an awkward assignment, because the word does not appear in the presented final decrypted text. However, I assume that is wrong and I have adjusted i, so the word 'paix' appears. Also, the assignment for *"ge"* is remarkable to say the least: nor 59, nor 'ge' occurs in the cipher, except 'gens' which is assigned to ~66. (DS)

The second reflection that can be made is that there is a particular link between the letters and the syllables, which composes a text, and that in the beginning we see some of them, and those that we recognize by others that are connected to them, which also could lead to new ones, but even when the first ones have been verified and show that those are correctly conjectured, still some "*postériori*" [80](as we learn in school) could show up, by for example the arrangement of the ciphered characters, or through the resulting text, but these first conjectures serve to find the other unknown characters in the beginning, as like knowing the effects by their cause. Whence it follows that the beginning of a decipherment operation (*à priori*) is not based only on appearances and similarities, but that the end of the same operation is becoming more certain each time we apply it there, until it contains a true demonstration.

From where we arrive at a certain point where we make the key of a cipher on a ciphered letter, the same key will be used to decipher without difficulty and without pain, all the other intercepted letters in the same correspondence, until the cipher key will be changed.

As it happens in the explanation of the effects of physics which itself are a real cipher for philosophers when it comes to the search for the causes, because when it comes to the explanation of the relation and uniformity of these certain effects, we imagine the cause, and we can say that we only know it afterwards (posteriori), by its effects.

But when we use the same cause as a principle already established that explains other effects of which we had not thought of before, and which nevertheless relate equally well, and is very constant then the proof is à priori, when one explains the effects by their real cause and it's no longer an assumption of the cause by the effects.

Thirdly it may be thought that since the art of decryption is mainly based on realities and assumptions, one need not to fear to make at first sight of appearance, because if the supposition is true, it will serve very well for the success of the search that one makes, so we will go to the point where we can verify true from false and compare all the other ciphered characters, whose true meaning must necessarily be incompatible with all the false assumptions, as like

---

[80] A *postériori* is a fact that we learn after the event took place. For example: the boy told afterwards that the dog was not kicked at all, but he stumbled over it himself. From newspaper.(DS)

the heights that are immeasurable in geometry [81] that can have no relation with the proportion of others. (61vo)

One can observe in the fourth place, that when one notices a big difference between the quality or the modification of the ciphered characters in a letter, it is a good indication that they form various columns and that they are to say of different kinds.

In such a way that we can assign one of the letters of the alphabet to them, other letters to the syllables and yet more others to proper words, which shines a little light and facilitates our work of decryption; we have seen the proof of this during the previous problem, where it was first seen that the numbers modified by two accents as like f.e.

       "   "   "

10   20   24

represent the single letters of the alphabet.

This is why we prepared, to tackle this weakness, a the cipher table that we proposed in our model for the Secretary of State, where we made sure that equal types of ciphered characters are being mixed within the various columns, such that there is no immediate appearance of these big differences to be seen.

Finally, the last reflection that can be made on this problem and also on the preceding ones is that the Art of decryption is not a certain indivisible secret which can be learned to another easily, like the secret to make the powder, to melt stones, to arrange the material for glass or crystal making, the secrets of extracting certain minerals, the ingredients of quintessence [82] and finally the secrets of chemistry and so many others that serve as principles in most arts which are in use, by which it is not necessary to reveal the secret to another person to show him how it works and become as skilful as the one who teaches it.

But it is not the same in the art of deciphering, especially with composite ciphers, because it is founded only in sustained reasoning, by a strong

---

[81] "comme les grandeurs que l'on appelle incommensurables dans la géométrie"
[82] During the Middle Ages, quintessence was the fifth element ((Aristotle), sometimes called aether, a most essential material in the universe besides earth, water, air, fire. (DS)

102

imagination, having several ideas in mind for all places where it is needed, will give reasons to discover the true meaning of what is true and what false, and finally, the result of certain principles and rules established by experience in relation to the genius of languages and the indispensable connection of speech.

From this all it follows that it isn't enough to establish axioms, to make observations, or even to give examples, as has been done here to show the method of deciphering; if one would make the application of it, which requires a great deal of time, attention, work, patience, and a good (if it must be said) and particular genius, and certain dispositions of characters, which seem sufficiently incompatible.

Chapter VIII: Decryption method for certain ciphers

(62vo) Sometimes they are used instead of numbers, the same letters of the alphabet that make up the words that one wants to disguise by presenting them only in another order and arbitrary disposition. Such that it confuses so much, that they no longer form sensible meaning unless they have been placed back into the order that they must have among themselves, to compose the narration which, one wished to write into cipher.

This is what is called encryption by figure, because the key of this cipher is nothing less than a certain figure of geometry, of which we will be convinced, like a square, a parallelogram, a triangle, etc., divided by as many cells as one wants, in which we put each in its rank the letters which form the narration.

After seeing them from another angle, by turning the figure to another side, one transcribes all these characters in the order of this new side of the figure, which changed the disposition much. In such a way that one recognizes there nothing any more than gibberish which is the cipher in question and the key will not be found unless one sees the same figure that formed the basis for that encryption.

In such case we can view the original text by turning the same figure to the same side as used. This method of encryption will be better explained by the example that we will show now by an easy narration.

i	l	e	r	r	f	h	q	n	n	m	e	r
l	u	d	c	l	d	i	u	e	s	e	u	e
e	s	i	e	a	e	f	e	n	e	l	a	u
s	a	n	p	c	c	f	l	e	c	o	f	o
t	y	t	t	l	e	r	o	p	o	n	a	i
p	s	e	e	e	c	e	n	e	m	l	i	r

If we go through each cell of this parallelogram[83] from top to bottom, starting with the first row, we will find these words: *"il est plus aysé d'intercepter la clef de ce chiffre que l'on ne pense, comme l'on va le faire voir."* [84] [85] (63vo)

---

[83] 13 rows x 6 columns is 78 cells in total (DS)

[84] "it is more likely that we intercept the key to this cipher than one thinks, as will be shown" (DS)

[85] In the original the text contained a small error and said: ..que l'on le pense.. , corrected that.(DS)

But if we consider the horizontal side, beginning from above, and we write the characters down from all cells, we get the following cipher: [86]

i.l.e.r.r.f.h.q.n.n.m.e.r. l.u.d.c.l.d.i.u.e.s.e.u.e.

e.s.i.e.a.e.f.e.n.e.l.a.u. s.a.n.p.c.c.f.l.e.c.o.f.o.

t.y.t.t.l.e.r.o.p.o.n.a.i. p.s.e.e.e.c.e.n.e.m.l.i.r.

Now, to discover the key to this cipher, we need not much mystery, nor the reasoning as we did on those before. It is only necessary to create a big square of forty or fifty cells on each side, and place all these characters in it, two by two in cells, or three by three, four by four squared, or as parallelogram; in many different ways that we finally find the true figure, which was used as key for the cipher, and the point that we notice that these letters are arranged such that they form a sensible meaning or at least a part of a sentence in the first column.

I have said that it was necessary to create a square cipher, a figure of forty or fifty cells, because it is the biggest one that is ordinarily used in these cases. However, if we do not find the true meaning through it, after placing all letters of the cipher in all different combinations and cells of the square, it would be necessary to create a larger one to tackle that problem, or create a large triangle instead of a square, in the same way and work on that in the same manner.

There is yet another more sophisticated way of discovering the key of this cipher without drawing any scheme. We only have to use the numbers from two until forty or fifty, that is to say that by assembling and by ordering and going through all these characters from the number two and upwards, it's infallible that we will see the true combination, because if the figure is regular, taking once every second character, once every third, every fourth, every fifth, and so on, until the we meet a combination that forms a meaning and finally words, it is necessary that we arrive there in the end.

But it must be noted that in this supposition we must always obey the first character and always use it on that position, which can be verified in the previous example, if we would take three characters we must always combine it with on the first position our first character.

---

[86] also notice that "va le faire voir", uses the letter U. and not the V. in the table (DS)

To find the figure of the triangle, it is necessary to perform the same movement, for example by always decreasing a number by another by taking for example the thirteenth character for the second (because the first is never changed and is always the first) the twelfth for the third, the eleventh for the fourth, the tenth for the fifth, and so on until they form the point of the triangle.

Chapter IX: decryption method for a special cipher

(64vo)

There is also a kind of cipher that is sometimes used in Holland, which seems to be indecipherable, because each character changes its meaning every time, depending on the condition of the word that serves as key for the ciphers. But it is difficult to form and use the method correctly, because the table which must be like that drawn on the other side of the page, on which the cipher is placed. At first the two parties must agree that a specific word serves as key and this could also be changed each time by mail, to make it more secure.

Now, the practice of this cipher is such: suppose that the key word is *"Amsterdam"* and that the word we want to cipher is *"Monsieur"*. We look at the table on the top and find the first letter of the key. In this case A. Then go down until we find the first letter of our plain text which we want to encrypt, in this case the M. At the intersection of the key column and the plain text row, we will find a number which is our cipher. In this example 11. See the table on the next page.

Then we move to the second letter and do the same; the second letter of the key is M. and the second letter of our plain text is O., which gives us 2. And so on for all letters until the letters of the key have been used. Then we start again at the beginning of the same keyword and continue with our plain text until the end. The cipher text now contains a big variation of characters, and never the same ciphered character signifies the same plain characters, unless by chance. (65vo)

Breaking this cipher is almost impossible, due to this variety that gives no clue for the decryption and on how to solve it, however, there is a small weakness that we can use, although it takes some time.

The method is to go over each of those numbers that are in the ciphered letter and match them with the twenty two letters of the alphabet, until a combination of a word or a half-word appears. Then we can fill the possible table with combinations that corresponds to that and allows to create another word.

After which it may be held as certain that this second found word will be the true key of the cipher, for it is certain that any other combination than the true one will only produce gibberish.

But it must necessarily result in a great deal of text because each digit must be compared with the 22 letters of the alphabet, this will take for each character $22^2 = 484$ comparisons. Since that this treatise is already too long, perhaps it is better to dispose this prolix. These kinds of ciphers are not very much used in the Secretaries because of their length and long time needed to encrypt and decrypt a message.

	A	B	C	D	E	F	G	H	I	L	M	N	O	P	Q	R	S	T	V	X	Y	Z
A	1	2	3	4	5	6	7	8	9	10	11	12	13	14	15	16	17	18	19	20	21	1
B	2	3	4	5	6	7	8	9	10	11	12	13	14	15	16	17	18	19	20	21	1	2
	A	B	C	D	E	F	G	H	I	L	M	N	O	P	Q	R	S	T	V	X	Y	Z
C	3	4	5	6	7	8	9	10	11	12	13	14	15	16	17	18	19	20	21	1	2	3
D	4	5	6	7	8	9	10	11	12	13	14	15	16	17	18	19	20	21	1	2	3	4
	A	B	C	D	E	F	G	H	I	L	M	N	O	P	Q	R	S	T	V	X	Y	Z
E	5	6	7	8	9	10	11	12	13	14	15	16	17	18	19	20	21	1	2	3	4	5
F	6	7	8	9	10	11	12	13	14	15	16	17	18	19	20	21	1	2	3	4	5	6
	A	B	C	D	E	F	G	H	I	L	M	N	O	P	Q	R	S	T	V	X	Y	Z
G	7	8	9	10	11	12	13	14	15	16	17	18	19	20	21	1	2	3	4	5	6	7
H	8	9	10	11	12	13	14	15	16	17	18	19	20	21	1	2	3	4	5	6	7	8
	A	B	C	D	E	F	G	H	I	L	M	N	O	P	Q	R	S	T	V	X	Y	Z
I	9	10	11	12	13	14	15	16	17	18	19	20	21	1	2	3	4	5	6	7	8	9
L	10	11	12	13	14	15	16	17	18	19	20	21	1	2	3	4	5	6	7	8	9	10
	A	B	C	D	E	F	G	H	I	L	M	N	O	P	Q	R	S	T	V	X	Y	Z
M	11	12	13	14	15	16	17	18	19	20	21	1	2	3	4	5	6	7	8	9	10	11
N	12	13	14	15	16	17	18	19	20	21	1	2	3	4	5	6	7	8	9	10	11	12
	A	B	C	D	E	F	G	H	I	L	M	N	O	P	Q	R	S	T	V	X	Y	Z
O	13	14	15	16	17	18	19	20	21	1	2	3	4	5	6	7	8	9	10	11	12	13
P	14	15	16	17	18	19	20	21	1	2	3	4	5	6	7	8	9	10	11	12	13	14
	A	B	C	D	E	F	G	H	I	L	M	N	O	P	Q	R	S	T	V	X	Y	Z
Q	15	16	17	18	19	20	21	1	2	3	4	5	6	7	8	9	10	11	12	13	14	15
R	16	17	18	19	20	21	1	2	3	4	5	6	7	8	9	10	11	12	13	14	15	16
	A	B	C	D	E	F	G	H	I	L	M	N	O	P	Q	R	S	T	V	X	Y	Z
S	17	18	19	20	21	1	2	3	4	5	6	7	8	9	10	11	12	13	14	15	16	17
T	18	19	20	21	1	2	3	4	5	6	7	8	9	10	11	12	13	14	15	16	17	18
	A	B	C	D	E	F	G	H	I	L	M	N	O	P	Q	R	S	T	V	X	Y	Z
V	19	20	21	1	2	3	4	5	6	7	8	9	10	11	12	13	14	15	16	17	18	19
X	20	21	1	2	3	4	5	6	7	8	9	10	11	12	13	14	15	16	17	18	19	20
	A	B	C	D	E	F	G	H	I	L	M	N	O	P	Q	R	S	T	V	X	Y	Z
Y	21	1	2	3	4	5	6	7	8	9	10	11	12	13	14	15	16	17	18	19	20	21
Z	1	2	3	4	5	6	7	8	9	10	11	12	13	14	15	16	17	18	19	20	21	1

Chapter X: Indecipherable ciphers

After having given the method for decryption of the ciphers which are ordinarily used, before finishing this treatise, it will not be out of place to say a thing on those ciphers that cannot be deciphered. It is not very difficult to recognize them, since by all that has been given in the preceding chapters it is easy to judge what are the indecipherable figures.

In fact, if the Art of decryption consists only in making suppositions and forming conjectures for thinking about plausibility's, and finally taking advantages of what seems to be the weakness in a cipher in order to discover the mystery of it, it follows from that if the key to the decryption is such that it leaves no room for suppositions nor does it provide any beginning for creation of conjectures, then it will be impossible to decrypt it. Unless it is composed with a symmetry and has a perfect proportion of numbers, such that the key of which we treated in the preceding chapter, of which we can say that the extreme symmetry takes the place of a weakness at the same time. And then it seems to be hidden by the variety of expressions of each character which changes in every occurrence. (66vo)

Now, it is certain that one of the elements of ciphers which has the necessary qualities to be indecipherable is the cipher that uses addition and subtraction. This is exercised in the following manner: we form a simple alphabet (because the simplest is the best for this kind of cipher)

A	B	C	D	E	F	G	H	I	L	M	N	O	P	Q	R	S	T	V	X	Y	Z
1	2	3	4	5	6	7	8	9	10	11	12	13	14	15	16	17	18	19	20	21	22

and we take a sentence from a text, a passage from the Holy Scripture or a expression from a daily prayers such from the Pater Noster or Ave Maria, etc. which will contain the key.

After having placed the characters of this expression on those of the text which one wants to encrypt, such a way that the first character is aligned to the first, the second to the second, etc.
We then make an addition of the two numbers, where the numbers below the characters signify the position in the table of the alphabet.

We put the result on the places of the simple cipher which means that each letter of the ciphered text as it is seen in this example where the key expression is the Pater Noster, etc. and the text that we want to encrypt is: "L'Armée est en marche,". The key has been arranged as we just have explained; and we will find the following, where the numbers that will make the result which signify each of the two characters that correspond to them, in the bottom row. [87]

P	A	T	E	R	N	O	S	T	E	R	Q	V	I	E	S	T
14	1	18	5	16	12	13	17	18	5	16	15	19	9	5	17	18
L	A	R	M	E	E	E	S	T	E	N	M	A	R	C	H	E
10	1	16	11	5	5	5	17	18	5	12	11	1	16	3	8	5
24	2	34	16	21	17	18	34	36	10	28	26	20	25	8	25	23

For the decryption it is necessary to subtract from each resulting number the digit which signifies the letter of the key, of course that corresponds to it and the remaining number which express the letter which one seeks.

For example, the first letter of the key is P. which signifies 14., then we subtract the 14. from the cipher that we have 24.-14.=10. which is the plain text, representing L which then is the first letter that we seek. The 2. is the second cipher letter, of which we subtract the value of the key A. which is one and gives one back for the second plain letter, and so on.

From this follows that with these kinds of keys we cipher by addition, and we decipher by subtraction, and as the numbers change at all signifying moments, and the key is not based on specific length, as in the example of the previous chapter, we can say that there is no method to intercept this key since we cannot give a set of fixes rules for it.

Another way of creating a key for an indecipherable cipher is this following one. First of all, we must make a list of all possible syllables and combinations of two and three letters such as *"abs, an, art,"* etc. , where it is not be necessary to use a specific alphabet. (67vo)

In the second place, all the numbers that signify each syllable must be made from three digits, that is above one hundred, and that they do not exceed that number, that is, they do not go beyond 999.

Thirdly, it is necessary to number on a separate paper the text that one wants to encrypt.

In the fourth place, from that paper we must transcribe the cipher that we are making differently, one part of the numbers with another part, according to the understanding for this cipher, which quite changes the order of the true cipher,

---

[87] In the original, the addition of the second last, 18+7, was mistakenly 26 (DS)

which will nevertheless remain the same to which it corresponds and all that were three digits. The following example will explain all that has been said here.

Assume that the ciphered characters on our paper will be

124. 256. 454.113. 414. 553. 364. 785. 256 etc.

To completely change the arrangement of the numbers and to set up a new trap for the decipherer and to deceive his conjectures and to frustrate his application, it will only be necessary to transcribe in the true cipher shipment; the separated numbers we have here but now give them another distance than before like

12. 42. 564. 541. 13. 41. 4. 55. 33. 64. 78. 52. 56.

where one can see it now forms another sequence, and there is no number anymore as it should be. The decipherer may try to discover what it means, but he will never come to the point where he understands it, because the numbers are not what they seem to be.

And yet whoever reveals the mystery will still have to replace them with their true meaning by dividing them in groups of three, by placing strokes in between, like this:
12. 4/2 . 56/4 . 54/1 . 13/41 . 4/55 . 3/3 . 64/78 . 5/2 . 56/ and by this method, the ciphered characters are getting back to their true form and give room for the discovery of their meaning with the help of the key.

But there are two disadvantages in using such kind of cipher: the first is that it requires a lot of time to encrypt it, since it must be placed on a separate paper before rearranging it and can send it how we want it in our cipher message.

The second disadvantage is that if one omits a single character, this single deflection changes the whole disposition of the ciphered article so that whoever has the key cannot decrypt its meaning. So that good application is necessary to make perfect use of this kind of indecipherable cipher.
Though the preceding appears to be impracticable in a Secretariat or at least in an ordinary and regulated correspondence, which this often involves too much delay on shipments during the use of these kinds of ciphers. (68vo)

We can still think of others, but these all have the same imperfections as those before, and it seems to be superfluous to make a more exact investigation, especially in a treatise that is not so much to satisfy the curiosity of the mind as to show the practical usage of ciphers.

Also, instead of trying to compose extraordinary ciphers, metaphysics, and those that are not good during use, it will always be better to use in the Secretaries the cipher tables and proper words[88], if one takes care to make them more ample than ordinary.

Increase the number of syllables of three letters, use a many null numbers, assign many cipher characters to the alphabet letters and to the syllables which repeated themselves often, so they can be diversified in the natural order of the ciphered numbers.

And finally, to observe all that has been proposed in parts of this treatise, where we have given the method of creation of the tables with ciphered characters and how that can be used well to make text more indecipherable.

All the observations which have been made in various parts of this work, are being very constant in detecting and deciding where the places are and which qualities a cipher must have, to make it not possible to intercept it, and we know how to perform well on all places which give reason to do so.

---

[88] I think he points here to nomenclators: words that are code for words (DS)

Appendix to chapter VII, second problem, Nijmegen interception 1676

In the treatise there were two different ciphered versions presented, these are:
 a) original book page 85 cipher, which we call the correct one
 b) original book page 73 cipher, with mistakes

In the latter, version b, there are twelve errors in total. The number 12. was changed into 13., and both represent the L. In it there are three cases where numbers are missing, and one occasion the position of a number was misplaced. The other mistakes were 56. (16), 65. (61), 75. (73). And then in four cases the diacritic used was wrong.

The published cipher in this appendix is based on the best version in the original, that is in the Chapter VII, second problem, which is a correct version. From that version, the exact decrypted transcription, with spaces added but without French diacritics, is as follows:

il nous a represente a plussieurs reprises qu'il ni avroit pas moyen de traiter ici sans paix si l'y estoit perpetuellement trouble parle bruit des armes que mesmes il seroit impossible de subcister si tout ce qui fait le pays de nimègue nestoit a couvert des courses et des violences des gens de guerre que nous y avions avtant dinterest que tous les autres ambassadeurs et qu'il nous prioit de le representer a votre masieste qu'il ni avoit encore avcuni contribution estallie dans toute lestendue du pays pour lequel on demande cette neutralite ainsi elle ni perdroit rien en accordant cette condetion et sans la-quelle il ni avoit pas lieu de croire que les ambassadeurs et ministres des prince et de leurs allies voulussent se rendre ici.

This text could not have been presented without the given solution which gave the words for the numbers, the so called 'nomenclatores', which probably never would have been solved without it. Examples of such words are: Prince, ambassadors, but also almost all syllables such as *"il, ver, interest, les, nous, qu'il, vou,"*etc. , that could not have been found without the presented solution.

The original text from the book was different in some instances and to give and idea of those, some lines are shown here of the two versions and the differences.

D=Decrypted text, Bk=original Book text.

D: il nous a represente ... de traiter ici sans paix
Bk   Il nous est représenté ... de traitter icy,

D: si l'y estoit ...
Bk   si l'on estoit ...

D: ... a votre masieste qu'il ni avoit encore avcuni contribution estallie
Bk   ... à Votre Ma.té   qu'il s'y avoit encore aucun contribution establie

D: ... ainsi elle ni perdroit rien
Bk   ... et qu'ainsy elle n'y perdrait rien

In some instances, the most convenient syllable is chosen, most often this is the most phonetical one. For example in "n'y", the nearest is "ni" and for "avcuni", which should have been "aucune", the "-ni" seems to be the most near for the encryptor at that time.

The decrypted text with columns for versions a) and b):

		a	b			a	b			a	b			a	b
IL	_	1		SI	..	71		B	,,	12		S	,,	38	
NOUS	_	67		L'	_	31		LE	_	19		DES	~	8	
A	,,	2		Y	,,	62		DE	~	1		GENS	~	66	
RE	..	44		ESTOIT	~	31		SU	..	75		DE	,	98	~
P	,,	16	56	PER	..	15		B	,,	12		GUERRE	~	68	miss.
RE	..	44		PE	_	99		Ci	,	75		QUE	..	24	
SE	..	69		TU	..	95		S	,,	38		NOUS	_	67	
N	,,	14		E	,,	6		TE	..	89		Y	,,	62	
TE	..	89		L	,,	13		R	,,	18		AV	,	39	
A	,,	2		LE	_	19		SI	..	71		i	,,	10	
PLUS	..	12		MENT	_	49		TOUT	..	97		ON	_	83	
SIE	~	94		T	,,	20	pos.	CE	,	73		S	,,	38	
U	,,	40		ROU	..	49		QUI	..	26		AV	,	39	
R	,,	18		B	,,	12		FAIT	~	46		TANT	^	4	
S	,,	38		LE	_	19		LE	_	19		D	,,	24	
RE	..	44		PAR	..	11		PA	_	96		INTEREST	_	11	
P	,,	16		LE	_	19		Y		31		QUE	..	24	
RI	..	46		B	,,	12		S	,,	38		TOU	..	94	
SE	..	69		RU	..	50		DE	,	98		S	,,	38	
S	,,	38		i	,,	10		Nimègue		124		LES	_	26	
QU'IL	..	34		T	,,	20		NEST	_	73	75	AUTRE	,	42	
NI	_	61	65	DE	,	98	^	OIT	_	89		S	,,	38	
AV	,	39		S		19		A	,,	2		ambassadeur		378	
ROIT	..	53		A	,,	2		COU	,	78		S	,,	38	
PAS	..	6		R	,,	18		VE	^	14		ET		32	
MOY	_	43		MES	_	46		R	,,	18	miss.	QU'IL	..	34	
E	,,	6		QUE	..	24		T	,,	20		NOUS	_	67	
N	,,	14		MES	_	46		DES	~	8		P	,,	16	
DE	,	98		MES	_	39		COUR	,	83		RI	..	46	
T	,,	20		IL	_	1		SE	..	69		OIT	_	89	
RA	..	43		SE	..	69		S	,,	38		DE	,	98	
i	,,	10		ROIT	..	53		ET		32		LE	,	68	
TE	..	89		i	,,	10		DES	~	8		RE	..	44	
R	,,	18		M	,,	32		VI	^	16		P	,,	16	
i	,,	10		PO	..	2		O		17		RE	..	44	
Ci	,	75		S	,,	38		LE	_	19		SE	..	69	
SANS	_	16		SI	..	71		N	,,	14		N	,,	14	
PAIX	..	14						CE	,	73					

	a	b			a	b			a	b			
TER	..	100		S	,,	38		CE	,	73		LEUR	_	29
A	,,	2		POUR	..	9		T	,,	20		S	,,	38
VOTRE	^	25		LE	_	19		TE	..	89		A	,,	2
MA	_	36		QUE	..	24		CON	,	81		L	,,	13
SIE	~	94		L	,,	13		DE	~	1		Li	_	21
S	,,	38		ON	_	83		TION	^	2		E	,,	6
TE	..	89		DE	,	98		ET	..	85		S	,,	44
QU'IL	..	34		MA	_	36		SANS	_	16		VOU	^	19
NI	_	61		N	,,	14		LA-QUELLE	..	35		LU	_	25
A	,,	2		DE	,	98		IL	_	1		S	,,	38
VOI	^	18		CE	,	73		NI	_	61		SE	..	69
T	,,	20		T	,,	20		A	,,	2		N	,,	14
EN	~	16		TE	..	89		VOI	^	18		T	,,	20
CO	,	76		NEUTR	_	75		T	,,	20		SE	..	69
RE	..	44		A	,,	2		PAS	..	6		RE	..	44
AV	,	39		Li	_	21		Li	_	21		N	,,	14
CU	,	79		TE	..	89		E	,,	6		D	,,	24
NI	_	59		AI	..	22		U	,,	40		RE	..	44
CON	,	81		N	,,	14		DE	,	98		i	,,	10
T	,,	20		SI	..	71		C	,,	4		Ci	,	75
RI	..	46		E	,,	6		RO	..	47				
BU	,	64		L	,,	13		i	,,	10				
TION	^	2		LE	_	19		RE	..	44				
EST	~	25		NI	_	59		QUE	..	24				
A	,,	2		PER	..	15		LES	_	26				
L	,,	12	13=L	D	,,	24		ambassadeur		378				
Li	_	21		ROIT	..	53		S	,,	38				
E	,,	6	miss.	RI	..	46		ET		32				
DANS	~	6		E	,,	6		MI	_	41				
TOUT	..	97		N	,,	14		NI	_	61				
E	,,	6		EN	~	16		S	,,	38				
LES	_	26		A	,,	2		T	,,	20				
TE	..	89		C	,,	4		RE	..	44				
N	,,	14		CO	,	76		S	,,	38				
DU	~	5		R	,,	18		DES	~	8				
F	,,	6		DA	,	95		Prince		193				
DU	~	5		N	,,	14		ET	,,	64				
PA	_	96		T	,,	20		DE	,	98				
Y	,,	62												

Looking only at the numbers used in the cipher, without the markings on their top/left, we see that the encryptor has a high preference for the numbers 38. 2. 14. 6. 20. (high to low).

IL NOUS A RE P RE SE N TE A PLUS SIE U R S RE P RI SE S QU'IL NI AV ROIT PAS MOY E N DE T RA i TE R i Ci SANS PAIX
1 67 2 44 16 44 69 14 89 2 12 94 40 18 38 44 16 46 69 38 34 61 39 53 6 43 6 14 98 20 43 10 89 18 10 75 16 14

SI L' Y ESTOIT PER PE TU E L LE MENT T ROU B LE PAR LE B RU i T DE S A R MES QUE MES MES IL SE ROIT i M PO S SI
71 31 62 31 15 99 95 6 13 19 49 20 49 12 19 11 19 12 50 10 20 98 19 2 18 46 24 46 39 1 69 53 10 32 2 38 71

B LE DE SU B Ci S TE R SI TOUT CE QUI FAIT LE PA Y S DE Nimègue NEST OIT A COU VE R T DES COUR SE S ET DES VI O LE N CE
12 19 1 75 12 75 38 89 18 71 97 73 26 46 19 96 31 38 98 124 73 89 2 78 14 18 20 8 83 69 38 32 8 16 17 19 14 73

S DES GENS DE GUERRE QUE NOUS Y AV i ON S AV TANT D INTEREST QUE TOU S LES AUTRE S ambass. S ET QU'IL NOUS P RI OIT DE LE RE P RE SE N
38 8 66 98 68 24 67 62 39 10 83 38 39 4 24 11 24 94 38 26 42 38 378 38 32 34 67 16 46 89 98 68 44 16 44 69 14

TER A VOTRE MA SIE S TE QU'IL NI A VOI T EN CO RE AV CU NI CON T RI BU TION EST A L Li E DANS TOUT E LES TE N DU E DU PA Y
100 2 25 36 94 38 89 34 61 2 18 20 16 76 44 39 79 59 81 20 46 64 2 25 2 12 21 6 6 97 6 26 89 14 5 6 5 96 62

S POUR LE QUE L ON DE MA N DE CE T TE NEUTR A Li TE AI N SI E L LE NI PER D ROIT RI E N EN A C CO R DA N T
38 9 19 24 13 83 98 36 14 98 73 20 89 75 2 21 89 22 14 71 6 13 19 59 15 24 53 46 6 14 16 2 4 76 18 95 14 20

CE T TE CON DE TION ET SANS LA-QUELLE IL NI A VOI T PAS Li E U DE C RO i RE QUE LES ambass. S ET MI NI S T RE S DES Prince ET DE
73 20 89 81 1 2 85 16 35 1 61 2 18 20 6 21 6 40 98 4 47 10 44 24 26 378 38 32 41 61 38 20 44 38 8 193 64 98

LEUR S A L Li E S VOU LU S SE N T SE RE N D RE i Ci
29 38 2 13 21 6 44 19 25 38 69 14 20 69 44 14 24 44 10 75

copyright DPJA SCHEERS 2019

If we sort all numbers with their diacritic markings, still ,,38. stays the highest.
Their counts are here displayed.

	repeats
,,38=S	18
,,20=T	12
,,2=A	11
,,14=N	11
44=RE	10
,,6=E	9
,98=DE	9
_19=LE	8
89=TE	8

Weakness

In the alphabetical table below can be clearly seen, that the weakness is this
cipher lies in the fact that characters with ,, (double quotes/double comma's) are
always single plain alphabet letters.

Letter frequency compared

Compared to the French language letter frequency, where the highest are
E.S.I.T.N. we get here S.T.A.N.
Now, we see that the vowels E. on 6. and the i. on 10. were only used nine and
seven times as separate letter; but most of the times they form a composite
syllable.
On the positive side, looking only at the highest counts on the consonants we
see that S.T.N. matches perfectly.

Bigrams

Removing the single letters, the top bigram are in correct order: RE. DE. LE. TE.
SE.
Looking at the French language bigrams, the top ones are: en.es.nt.re.le.er.oi.
At first sight only the LE. RE. seems equal and shows clearly that this does not
work for composite (short) ciphers.

Here is the alphabetical list of the unique cipher characters used:

,,2=A	22=AI	_25=LU	^16=VI	^19=VOU	^25=VOTRE
,,12=B	,39=AV	_36=MA	,81=CON	,83=COUR	~31=ESTOIT
,,4=C	,64=BU	_41=MI	,78=COU	~6=DANS	~68=GUERRE
,,24=D	,73=CE	_59=NI	~8=DES	~46=FAIT	193=Prince
,,6=E	,75=Ci	_61=NI	~25=EST	~66=GENS	124=Nimègue
,,10=i	,76=CO	_83=ON	_26=LES	_29=LEUR	_11=INTEREST
,,12=L	,79=CU	_96=PA	_39=MES	_49=MENT	35=LA-QUELLE
,,13=L	,95=DA	_99=PE	_46=MES	_73=NEST	378=ambassadeur
,,32=M	,98=DE	2=PO	_43=MOY	_67=NOUS	
,,14=N	~1=DE	43=RA	_89=OIT	14=PAIX	
17=O	~5=DU	44=RE	11=PAR	12=PLUS	
,,16=P	~16=EN	46=RI	6=PAS	9=POUR	
,,18=R	32=ET	47=RO	15=PER	53=ROIT	
19=S	85=ET	50=RU	24=QUE	_16=SANS	
,,38=S	,,64=ET	69=SE	26=QUI	^4=TANT	
,,44=S	_1=IL	71=SI	49=ROU	^2=TION	
,,20=T	_31=L'	75=SU	~94=SIE	97=TOUT	
,,40=U	,68=LE	89=TE	100=TER	,42=AUTRE	
31=Y	_19=LE	95=TU	94=TOU	_75=NEUTR	
,,62=Y	_21=Li	^14=VE	^18=VOI	34=QU'IL	

Further observations

There is the relation that ciphers with ,, represent the single plain characters.
Exceptions seems to be ,,64 =ET. and 17=O. 19=S. 31=Y. In total there are 20
single characters, of which some doubles for L. S. Y.

The F.G.H.J.K.Q.V.W.X.Z letters are not used as single character, as a result only
<u>seventeen</u> letters of the alphabet have been used as single letter. During that
period French used the alphabet consisting of 22 letters as displayed previously
in the book.

The three-digit ciphers represent important names or long words used in
diplomatic traffic (Prince, Nimègue, ambassadeur).

Letter-digit-relation, pro and contra

The proposed relation between digits on the left and plain text similarities, can
be found often, but it was not used always. We also show now some contra
dictionary examples, although these are less frequent.   For such letter-digit-
relation to example can be mentioned:

<u>pro</u>

,76=CO

,79=CU

,95=DA

,98=DE

_96=PA

_99=PE

_21=Li

_25=LU

_41=MI

_43=MOY

_46=MES

_49=MENT

<u>contra</u>

~16=EN

..85=ET

,,64=ET

..69=SE

..71=SI

47=RO

49=ROU

50=RU

53=ROIT

22=AI

24=QUE

Lastly, some general counts on the text:

spaces used:	none
total no. cipher characters:	285
total no. unique cipher characters:	109
in cipher, used plain single letters:	20
,, 2-grams:	41
,, 3-grams:	20
,, 4-grams:	16
,, 5-grams:	4

Appendix: Letter frequencies of English, French, Spanish, Dutch

Some basic letter frequencies of languages are displayed here for your convenience, based on medieval texts. Of course, depending on the length and subject of the text these statistics may change. Also, some top words are given as well as the bigrams, trigrams and quadgrams.

The _xx shows a piece of text that is at the _beginning of a word and the xx_ is at the end_ of a word.

top words			
English	Dutch	French	Spanish
the	en	et	y
and	de	de	de
of	van	il	a
in	zijn	la	el
it	het	à	que
a	hij	les	la
to	tot	le	en
is	in	en	su
or	zij	l	los
with	ik	que	tierra
are	een	d	dijo
as	zeide	dit	se
for	dat	qui	por
them	hem	je	no
that	den	des	del
be	gij		tu

English			2-gram	3-gram	4-gram
e	14,6%		e_	_th	and_
t	8,1%		th	he_	_and
o	7,4%		_t	the	_the
a	7,3%		he	nd_	the_
n	7,0%		s_	and	_of_
h	6,6%		_a	_an	_to_
s	6,5%		d_	is_	hat_
i	6,1%		an	of_	_in_
r	5,6%		t_	_of	that
d	4,6%		_h	_he	e_an
l	3,9%		n_	at_	_tha
y	2,6%		_s	e_a	his_
u	2,5%		nd	to_	_for
f	2,5%		er	es_	for_
m	2,4%		_w	re_	_he_
w	2,3%		re	_to	_is_
c	2,2%		_o	er_	e_th
g	1,7%		r_	en_	e_of
b	1,5%		_i	_in	_it_
p	1,4%		is	e_t	n_th
þ	1,3%		in	_hi	_his
k	0,7%		en	hat	ther
v	0,7%		de	de_	che_
z	0,2%		ha	in_	he_s
?	0,2%		or	e_h	s_an

Dutch		2-gram	3-gram	4-gram
e	23,2%	en	en_	ende
n	11,2%	e_	nde	nde_
d	7,5%	n_	de_	_end
t	6,9%	de	end	die_
a	6,2%	_d	_en	_die
i	6,0%	er	er_	den_
r	5,2%	t_	et_	dat_
s	4,8%	ie	_di	en_d
o	4,5%	nd	ie_	_dat
l	3,6%	_e	die	_van
m	2,8%	te	n_d	van_
h	2,4%	_s	_da	men_
c	2,3%	et	e_d	ten_
g	2,2%	an	den	en_e
v	2,0%	ge	_me	n_en
u	1,6%	di	dat	en_s
w	1,5%	_m	at_	der_
b	1,2%	me	an_	de_d
p	1,1%	r_	_de	_in_
k	1,0%	in	men	e_en
z	0,7%	_h	van	ren_
y	0,7%	ne	_va	n_di
f	0,5%	da	in_	_men
j	0,4%	_v	der	e_da
¶	0,2%	oe	_ge	aer_
q	0,1%	re	ne_	gen_
x	0,0%	at	ten	n_de
&	0,0%	_w	n_e	nen_
		es	n_s	en_v
		_g	_he	e_di
		al	e_s	en_m
Dutch		_a	te_	nder
1400-1500		s_	t_d	_den
		se	e_e	_sal
		le	ere	ande

French		2-gram	3-gram	4-gram
e	15,8%	e_	nt_	_et_
s	8,0%	t_	et_	_de_
i	7,7%	s_	_de	ent_
t	7,7%	en	es_	_en_
n	7,4%	_e	ent	que_
r	7,2%	es	_et	ant_
a	7,1%	_d	_qu	oit_
o	6,4%	nt	_en	_est
u	5,6%	_l	de_	_le_
l	5,4%	_a	en_	_il_
d	3,1%	re	_le	_que
c	2,9%	n_	le_	_ne_
m	2,9%	_p	it_	_la_
p	2,3%	_s	re_	qui_
v	1,8%	le	ne_	les_
q	1,4%	er	est	t_de
f	1,2%	oi	ant	e_de
g	1,1%	_c	que	_par
b	0,9%	de	_es	tre_
é	0,7%	i_	il_	_qui
h	0,7%	on	oit	est_
z	0,6%	r_	e_l	_li_
j	0,6%	et	e_d	e_et
y	0,5%	qu	ue_	ont_
x	0,3%	_m	s_e	_les
è	0,2%	an	_se	_son
à	0,2%	ie	t_l	t_le
ï	0,1%	a_	ien	_con
-	0,1%	l_	t_d	son_
ç	0,1%	ou	_il	ien_
		ai	_co	s_de
	French	or	us_	bien
	1100-1500	st	st_	ment
		ne	on_	s_et
		me	ns_	t_qu

Spanish		2-gram	3-gram	4-gram
e	13,5%	e_	_de	_de_
a	12,4%	a_	_y_	que_
o	8,9%	s_	os_	_el_
s	7,8%	_d	de_	_que
r	6,4%	o_	el_	_la_
n	5,7%	y_	que	los_
l	5,3%	_e	_el	_en_
d	5,1%	_a	ue_	s_de
i	5,1%	de	_la	_su_
u	4,2%	_s	_a_	a_de
t	3,9%	os	as_	_los
c	3,0%	_l	ra_	s_y_
m	3,0%	en	la_	ijo_
y	2,7%	_y	_qu	_hij
h	1,9%	n_	_en	_con
p	1,8%	ra	_su	o_de
b	1,7%	er	_se	a_y_
j	1,3%	es	es_	ron_
v	1,2%	ue	_di	_tie
q	1,1%	el	en_	os_d
ó	1,1%	_h	re_	_por
g	0,8%	la	s_d	e_la
í	0,8%	_t	_lo	o_y_
f	0,5%	l_	_ha	de_l
z	0,4%	_c	e_e	_est
ñ	0,4%	re	los	e_de
x	0,0%	_p	ier	_dij
k	0,0%	as	_co	a_ti
w	0,0%	_m	ent	erra
		an	e_l	tier
		ar	ijo	dijo
Spanish		ie	do_	ierr
1569		qu	on_	_del
		on	_es	hijo
		se	a_d	_y_l

Further reading

This list provides some interesting cryptography titles for further reading.

- Agostino Amadi. Trattato delle cifre. 1588. Trattato delle cifre.
- Aloys Meister, Die Anfänge der modernen diplomatischen Geheimschrift, 1902
- Meister. Die Geheimschrift im Dienste der Päpstlichen Kurie von Ihren Anfängen bis zum Ende des XVI jahrhunderts, by Aloys Meister, 1866. German.
- Pasini. Written Ciphers Used By The Republic Of Venice, Luigi Pasini, 1872, translated 2021 by D.P.J.A. Scheers. Amazon.com. Link.
- Zealous with Language and Ciphers, Shorthand, ciphers and universal language around the 17th century. D.P.J.A. Scheers. English, 250 pages. 2021.

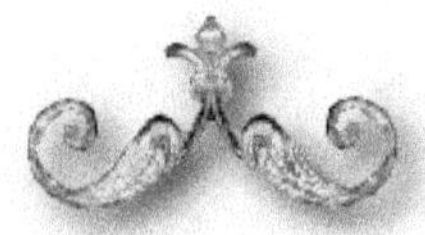

www.ingramcontent.com/pod-product-compliance
Lightning Source LLC
Chambersburg PA
CBHW051428150726
48000CB00005B/2004